'This is a great book: readable, practical and, most importantly, compassionate.

'Sarah Rayner gives a clear explanation of the common symptoms of anxiety and panic that affect so many lives. She then goes on to give sound advice as to how to cope with these ongoing feelings. This entails a series of strategies that encourage understanding of the anxiety rather than its suppression, aiming to give control of these complex emotions back to the patient. I will be recommending this book.'

Dr Patrick Fitzgerald, GP

'Sarah's advice is very sage. She encourages the reader to be kinder to themselves, live in the moment, and accept their anxiety as an occasionally troublesome, yet integral part of their own being. Deeply personal, yet eminently practical, this accessible and engaging book should prove extremely helpful to anyone trying to cope with anxiety.'

Dr Ian Williams, GP and author

'A self-help book packed with tips, exercises, and insights to ease worry and panic, this reads like chatting with an old friend; one with wit, wisdom and experience. Perfect for anyone suffering from this difficult disorder.'

The Book Doctor, Brighton and Hove Independent

Cover image: Madelyn Mulvaney
Design: Sarah Rayner

Non-fiction by Sarah Rayner:

Making Friends with Depression:
A warm and wise companion to recovery

More Making Friends with Anxiety:
A little book of creative activities to help
reduce stress and worry

Making Friends with Anxiety:
A Calming Colouring Book

Making Friends with the Menopause:
A clear and comforting guide to support
you as your body changes

Novels by Sarah Rayner:

Another Night, Another Day
The Two Week Wait
One Moment, One Morning
Getting Even
The Other Half

SARAH RAYNER

Making Friends with Anxiety

with photographs
by the author

Hello and welcome

Hot sweats, palpitating heart, shaking limbs, racing thoughts – to live with anxiety can be very distressing. In excess, anxiety can stop you doing lots of things – sometimes *anything*. It can make you irritable and angry or sad and depressed (anxiety and depression are often linked) and interfere with relationships, work and your physical health. Anxiety is also one of the most common forms of mental ill-health in the world so, if you suffer from it, you're not alone, and I hope this book goes some way to helping you feel connected with others going through something similar. But before we open this particularly wriggly can of worms, allow me to introduce myself and explain how I came to write *Making Friends with Anxiety*.

About me

I'm Sarah Rayner, and my day (and sometimes night) job is as an author – some of you might have come by this via the bestselling *One Moment, One Morning,* or the follow-up novels, *The Two Week Wait* and *Another Night, Another Day.*

'What qualifies a novelist to write about anxiety?' you might ask.

The answer is simple: 'I've been there.'

At various times, anxiety has stopped me being able to work, interfered with my relationships and zapped my confidence. Over the years I've tried many different kinds of medication and therapy, and much has helped, but in 2012 I had a bout so bad that it seemed nothing would alleviate my symptoms, so I admitted myself to a clinic specialising in anxiety as a day patient. It was there, amongst fellow sufferers, that I learned how to manage my anxiety properly.

I'm still affected by anxiety from time to time, but to a significant extent I've come out the other side, so in 2014 I decided to write this little book as a companion for others seeking support. Since then many thousands of people around the world have read it, and my other *Making Friends with Anxiety* titles (*A Calming Colouring Book* and *A Little Book of Creative Activities*) too, which just shows how common anxiety is. I've updated this edition for 2016, but its essence and my intention remains the same: I hope reading it feels like a chat with a good friend, and that it helps you as much as what I've learned has helped me.

About this book

There are other books available on anxiety, some good, so why bother reading this one?

1.   **Making anxiety the enemy will exacerbate the condition, so befriending anxiety is your best tactic**. It might surprise you to learn that anxiety isn't a bad thing *per se*. In many ways it can actually serve us. It can help alert us to the fact we might be taking too much on and that we have to look after ourselves, for example. So we need anxiety, just as we need laughter and tears and friends and family. Have you heard the saying, 'Keep your friends close, and your enemies closer'? It is a useful one to bear in mind, as it pretty well describes my approach here.

2.   **This book is written with honesty**. I won't make false promises – *Making Friends with Anxiety* isn't going to *cure* your anxiety. I don't believe in miracles, and to my mind anyone who suggests they can get rid of your anxiety forever is talking claptrap. Let me be clear from the off: whether you experience full-blown panic attacks, suffer from a phobia or live with worry gnawing away at your insides every day, you won't ever be shot of anxiety entirely. Your anxiety – like mine – is here to stay. But

whereas hitherto panic and fear had often controlled me, these days you could say that anxiety occupies a space in my life rather like an annoying flatmate; one who doesn't do the washing up or put the loo seat down. My anxiety gremlin is there; he can't always be ignored, and some days he really irks me, but he doesn't really do me any harm, or curtail how I choose to spend my time. Moreover, I have learned that trying to fight anxiety will, in all likelihood, make it worse, and in this little book I'll explain why.

3.   **Anxiety manifests itself differently in all of us.** Some might get obsessed with checking things over and over, others may feel overwhelmed by intrusive thoughts. But whilst I might not have experienced anxiety in exactly the same way as you, I do have first-hand knowledge of panic so crushing I've been pinned to the floor by fear. I'm an expert on anxiety – my *own* anxiety – and I hope to help you become the same: an expert on your own anxiety.

4.   **I don't have an axe to grind.** I'm not affiliated to any one doctrine; I'm not a practising Buddhist, or a medic, or a therapist. I'm just keen to share much of what has

worked – and continues to work – for me, and I've included some of my own experiences in what follows. That's not to say I haven't drawn on other people's expertise – I have. I've been in therapeutic groups and benefitted hugely from talking to fellow sufferers and hearing their stories. It was largely because I've found groups useful myself that at the same time that I published this book, I also set up **a group on Facebook** (called *Making Friends with Anxiety*, too) where we – and you if you wish – can share experiences and support one another in confidence. The group now has thousands of members and numbers continue to grow, and I've included members' insights in this updated edition, without naming anyone in full to maintain confidentiality. There is also a list of websites and further recommended reading at the end, which I hope will give you more tools to use in your recovery.

Photo (as on cover): Madelyn Mulvaney

5.   **The format of this book is designed with anxiety in mind**. It's relatively short and comes in bite-sized chunks, because I don't know about you, but when I'm anxious I have the attention span of goldfish. You'll find

exercises so you can put the theories into practice, but if you just want to dip in, you'll find quick tips and useful insights in italics and the main points emphasized in bold. Should you feel really wobbly, I suggest you head for this highlighted text as then you'll have less to digest. In this edition I've included a page at the end of each chapter for your own notes or you can doodle in the space if you prefer.

6. **Each chapter focuses on one component of anxiety to make it easier to remember what you've read**. Together the seven chapters make up the word 'A.N.X.I.E.T.Y.' – starting with 'A' for Adrenaline and finishing with 'Y' for You. This simple format is designed to make it easier to recall the advice in this book when you've finished it.

7. **By the time you've finished this book, I hope you will have gained a good overview of the common causes of anxiety and be well on the way to being less anxious yourself**. I wish you all the best on your journey.

Contents

Introduction

- What exactly *is* anxiety?
- Investing in your own wellbeing
- Different kinds of anxiety

1. A is for Adrenaline

To see anxiety as purely a disease of the mind is simplistic because when we're anxious we respond by releasing the hormone adrenaline, which produces a chain of reactions throughout the entire nervous system. In treating anxiety, the body is thus a good place to start.

- Physical symptoms of anxiety
- The link between fear and anxiety
- Looking after our bodies
- Medication, the options in a nutshell
- Making friends with your doctor
- Therapeutic treatments in brief
- The value of physical exercise
- The role of diet and drink
- The importance of breathing
- The physical changes of the menopause

2. N is for Negative Thoughts

Self-criticism, perfectionism and impatience can feed anxiety. Becoming aware of negative thought patterns and learning to challenge them can reduce overwhelm.

- Negative thinking
- Changing our minds
- Handling criticism
- Perfectionism
- Common negative patterns of thought

3. X is for X-factor

Some situations will make particular individuals worry more than others, and are thus the 'X-factor' – variable component – in our personal experience of anxiety. Learning what triggers us can provide perspective.

- The personal nature of anxiety
- Past experience and triggers
- Seeking professional help

4. I is for Imagination

Imagining the worst about what has yet to happen can play a large part in anxiety so it's important to learn how to let go and be more objective.

- Common imaginative patterns of thought
- Ways to tackle worry
- Insomnia and the imagination

5. E is for Escalation

Anxiety leads many of us to adopt ways of behaving so we won't feel overcome by fear, but these coping strategies often only offer short-term relief, and in the long term cause anxiety to escalate. Learning to face our fears is a key.

- Common coping mechanisms
- Drugs and alcohol
- Avoidance
- The vicious circle
- Breaking the vicious circle
- Changing behaviour
- Stepping stones
- Your personal survival kit

6. T is for Time

We create anxiety by worrying about the future and mulling over the past, yet we can't control the former or change the latter. Discovering how to live more in the 'now' is time well spent.

- Stop the planet, I want to get off
- Follow a furry friend's lead
- Gaining perspective

7. Y is for You

By understanding more about your mind and body and changing the way you approach fear, *you* can manage your own anxiety, rather than your anxiety managing you.

- Being your own best friend
- A balanced life
- A – Y, a summary of the tools at your fingertips
- For times of need

Introduction

0.1 What exactly *is* anxiety?

Anxiety has many potential causes and degrees.
Personally, it's a word I'd use to describe feeling nervous
and scared, accompanied by butterflies in my tummy and
shakiness. This is how I experience more mild anxiety, and
when it's at this level I can usually cope OK. But if these
symptoms escalate and I get dizzy, then I can start to panic,
and when I panic, I feel my heart palpitating, which then
makes my anxiety worse. Soon I'm caught in a vicious circle
where my thoughts are whirling and it's hard to function.

**Doubtless you'll have your own sense of anxiety,
as the way it manifests itself is different for each of us and
varies day to day.** Should you join the *Making Friends with
Anxiety* Facebook group, you'll soon see, as I have, not just
how widespread anxiety is, but also how it impacts each of
us in a distinct way. Much has also been written and said
about the 21st century being a time of high anxiety
historically, and whether or not this is true, what is certain
is that we *all* worry sometimes. I bet even the Dalai Lama
has the odd anxious moment – it's part of being human.

So if everyone experiences anxiety, when does it
become a problem? There's no easy answer to this, but **if
your anxiety is seriously curtailing your day-to-day
enjoyment of life, then it's worth exploring ways of
lessening the hold it has on you.**

Inevitably, there will be situations when we're more
susceptible to being anxious, just as certain events mean
we're more likely to be sad, and the two often go hand in
hand. Bereavement, illness, losing a job, divorce – all these
stresses can heighten anxiety to a point we've not
experienced before. Many of us get more anxious with age

as we worry about our health and frailty, and physical transitions such as the menopause can heighten anxiety. But however old we are and whatever experiences we've had, it's often not easy to talk about anxiety, especially when we're in the midst of a bad bout of it, as our thoughts become tangled and expressing ourselves is hard.

Some signs that we are very anxious are:

- Excessive worry or fear
- Refusing to do routine activities or being overly preoccupied with routine
- Avoiding social situations
- Being overly concerned with safety
- Hoarding/collecting
- Self-medicating with alcohol or overeating
- A racing heart, shallow breathing, trembling, nausea, sweating
- Muscle tension, feeling weak and shaky

You can probably can see that some of these relate to how we **think** and **feel** (we worry and are afraid, for instance), some to how we **behave** (self-medicating with excess alcohol or food) and some to the **physical** symptoms (a racing heart and feeling shaky).

In *Making Friends with Anxiety* we'll be learning how **all of these thoughts patterns, emotions, behaviours and physical sensations are connected.** Whilst this might sound complicated, it's actually good news, because **if we tackle one issue we may well find other symptoms improve too.**

0.2 Investing in your own wellbeing

'But I've so much to do, I haven't the *time* to deal with my anxiety,' you might protest. You may reason you're too busy looking after your kids or an elderly relative, or that everyone suffers from stress, and lying awake night after night churning over what's happening at work isn't that big a deal. Please don't get me wrong: I'm not advocating that you trample ruthlessly over others in a bid to look after yourself or that you set aside years to study the subject. But surely it's worth investing *some* time in your own wellbeing? After all, **if you're less anxious and happier, you'll be better placed to engage with other people and contribute socially, at work and with your loved ones**.

'The perfect man of old looked after himself before looking to help others.' Zhuang Zhou

This little book can be read in an hour or two, and I'd argue that's not a huge outlay of time when weighed against months or possibly years of suffering. This equation holds true no matter what form your anxiousness takes, which brings me onto the different kinds of anxiety.

18

0.3 Different kinds of anxiety

There are as many forms of anxiety as there are people on the planet and there is no doubt that sometimes labels can be limiting. Nonetheless, it's useful to be aware of the most common terms used by doctors and therapists giving a diagnosis of anxiety. You may recognize elements of your own experience in the definitions here and feel empowered by gaining clarity, and one sufferer explains more about the benefits she gained from getting a diagnosis in Chapter 3.

• **Post-Traumatic Stress Disorder** (PTSD) is usually triggered by one specific, very stressful and frightening event. PTSD can result from the experiences of war; traumatic incidents such as a mugging, rape, abuse, car accidents; or natural disasters such as floods or earthquakes. Symptoms may emerge months or years after the event and take the form of flashbacks or nightmares.

• **Obsessive Compulsive Disorder** (OCD) is when unwanted and unpleasant thoughts, images or urges repeatedly enter a person's mind. Often people feel compelled to behave in certain ways. Some are preoccupied with repeatedly checking things, touching things in a particular order, or counting things. Others are fixated by order, symmetry or hoarding unneeded items.

• **Generalized Anxiety Disorder** (GAD) is when people feel anxious in a wide range of situations and find it hard to pin-point why. Those with GAD can be overly concerned about health issues, money, family problems, or possible disaster.

• Those with **Panic Disorder** have sudden attacks of terror, and usually a pounding heart, chest pain, sweatiness, weakness, faintness, dizziness, or nausea. Panic attacks can occur at any time, even during sleep. An attack usually peaks within 10 minutes, but some symptoms may last longer. Sometimes someone experiencing a panic attack may believe he or she is having a heart attack or stroke.

•   A **phobia** is an extreme fear of an animal, object, place or situation. Some common phobias include **social phobia** (or social anxiety) – when an individual feels overwhelmingly anxious and self-conscious in everyday social situations, **agoraphobia** – a fear of being in places where escape might be difficult, and **claustrophobia** – a fear of enclosed spaces.

This is by no means an exhaustive list and I won't promise to cover off every condition in detail, but if you suffer from an anxiety disorder or anxiety-related symptoms, I hope you'll find this book helpful.

First, let's look at the origins of anxiety in terms of biology. Once we've shed some light on that, we'll understand what causes many of the physical effects of anxiety and begin to feel better.

A space for your own notes...

...or just to breathe

1. 'A' is for Adrenaline

If we're anxious we respond by releasing the hormone adrenaline, which produces a chain of reactions throughout the entire nervous system. To see anxiety as purely a disease of the mind is simplistic because it has so many physical symptoms.

When we treat anxiety, the body is thus a good place to start. What we put into our bodies – or avoid – in terms of food and drink can make a big difference. Gentle exercise can also help, as can slow, measured breathing.

1.1 Physical symptoms of anxiety

The majority of people who become anxious in stressful situations experience some of these physical symptoms:

- Increased heart rate
- Headaches
- Dizziness
- Blurred vision
- Dilation of the pupils
- Difficulty swallowing
- Dry mouth
- Nausea and/or vomiting
- Tingling
- Blushing
- Sweating
- Numbness
- Difficulty breathing
- Muscle contraction such as tightness in the neck, shoulders, chest and hands
- Indigestion
- Diarrhoea

- IBS
- Frequent urination

'Help,' you could be forgiven for thinking. 'That's a pretty worrying list.' You might find just reading about the symptoms seems to bring some of them on.

It's easy to get caught up in a cycle of worry and start to panic about the bodily sensations of anxiety. Time and again I've seen new members in our Facebook group panic about various physical symptoms and ailments, and whilst I wouldn't wish to discourage anyone from getting checked out by their doctor, I long to reassure them all that they will be probably be OK. One of the most comforting breakthroughs I had when learning to manage my anxiety was when I finally grasped that what I'd hitherto believed were serious, life-threatening conditions were, in fact, related to the fight/flight reflex which is part of our biological make-up. In other words **all these physical symptoms are quite normal.**

TIP: 'Research is key. If you understand what is happening to your body when you're having an anxiety attack then it makes the experience less frightening.' Rachel

1.2 The link between fear and anxiety

It would be unusual, wouldn't it, *not* to worry during exams or be alarmed by the prospect of having to give a speech at a wedding? Moreover, **in some situations, these responses are actively** *helpful* – imagine being threatened by an aggressive animal. Here the burst of adrenaline would bring about a much-needed 'fight or flight' response, useful if you needed to escape from a hungry lion. This is because **anxiety is connected to fear.** In fact, it can be said that

anxiety is the biological vestige of fear, the basic survival mechanism that helps safeguard us against danger. **We need fear, however horrible it feels to be afraid**.

- **When we experience fear, we get a rush of adrenaline**. The brain sends a biochemical message to the pituitary gland, which releases a hormone which triggers the adrenal gland to release adrenaline and noradrenaline.
- It's all systems go – **our breathing becomes faster and shallower**, supplying more oxygen to the muscles.
- **Our hearts beat more rapidly and blood is driven to the brain and limbs** so we can make split-second decisions and a quick getaway. This is why we experience heart palpitations, chest pains and tingling.
- **Blood is taken from areas of the body where it's not needed** like the stomach, because in a life-threatening situation, you're not going to stop for food. Thus when you're afraid, you may feel sick and unable to eat.
- **The liver releases stored sugar to provide fuel for energy.** Excess sugar in the blood can cause indigestion.

- **Muscles at the opening of the anus and bladder are relaxed.** Food and liquid are evacuated so you're lighter to run. Hence diarrhoea and frequent urination.
- **The body cools itself by perspiring.** Blood vessels and capillaries move close to the skin surface, leading to sweating and blushing.

Anxiety is your body signalling something is not quite right and if we experience these responses in a normal situation such as in a supermarket or business meeting, it can be very frightening. Often these physical symptoms arise together – a panic attack can involve difficulty in breathing, palpitations, dizziness and chest pains, for instance. Yet whilst panic attacks are scarier than nausea or diarrhoea, *all* these symptoms are connected to the release of adrenaline and are not problematic in themselves.

TIP: 'When I broke my wrist and had a plaster cast, everyone would say "what have you done?" because they could see it. The irony was that whilst it was a nuisance having the cast, it didn't really worry me. In many ways suffering from panic attacks was worse. I call anxiety "the invisible illness" because others weren't aware how tiring it was trying not to show how I was battling inside. Now I'm in the group online, I have somewhere I can share without feeling judged. Although I'm not cured, I feel better.' Val

Anxiety is only a problem when it becomes out of proportion, persistent or appears for no apparent reason, and arises when adrenaline production is triggered in response to situations where we don't actually *need* to run away or fight for survival. In other words, although we live in world where most of us aren't in mortal danger very often, evolution hasn't quite caught up with current lifestyles. In war zones it's different, sadly, but for the more fortunate amongst us, brushes with death are relatively few and far between. However in an anxious person, the body reacts as if there are still hungry lions round every corner.

It's also worth pointing out here that, as far as we know, **anxiety is a uniquely** human experience. Animals can experience fear in response to a perceived threat or danger, but *not* anxiety. Broadly speaking, this is because **animals live in the moment far more than humans do.** The *Medical Dictionary* differentiates fear and anxiety thus:

- **Fear is a direct, focused response to a specific event or object, and we are consciously aware of it.**
- **Anxiety involves the ability to use memory and the imagination to move backwards and forwards in time** in a way that other animals can't.

As a result, anxiety is often hard to pin to a specific cause. It reflects a combination of biochemical body changes, our individual personal history and memory, and the social situation. It could be said that **fear is a reminder that we were once cave dwellers who had to hunt for food and fight for survival. Yet as we've evolved and threats to our survival have morphed and bypassed our rational mind, so anxiety – not fear – has taken hold.**

Because anxiety is connected to our ability as human beings to conceive of time, **one of the most effective ways of calming the anxious mind is to become more 'animal'**, so to speak. When other mammals experience fear and have a rush of adrenaline, they don't analyse their symptoms – a cat being chased by a large dog is unlikely to pause; he just high-tails it. At its simplest, this is because our pets live in the present. When we follow their example and let go of ruminating on the past and worrying about the future and focus on the here and now, anxiety lessens.

26

TIP: 'I find it helps calm me when I'm anxious to give my kitty a snuggle and a stroke. It encourages me to focus on something else other than all the thoughts racing in my mind. It's lovely when you get some purrs back in appreciation and makes you feel loved even when you don't feel very loveable.' Lisa

We'll come back to the practice of living in the present moment, which is also known as *Mindfulness*, in Chapter 6. Meanwhile let's get back to the subject in hand – our bodies, and how caring for ourselves physically can help manage anxiety.

1.3 Looking after our bodies

I'm not a personal trainer, neither am I a nutritionist, but to write about managing anxiety *without* emphasising how important it is to look after ourselves physically would be a serious omission.

It's not hard to deduce from the list of symptoms in the introduction why **experiencing long-term anxiety can**

be detrimental to our health. It can contribute to heart disease, stomach ulcers, irritable bowel syndrome, migraine, back pain and rashes, and make us more likely to succumb to viruses like colds and flu. It's also linked to depression; one can bring on the other, as I found myself.

But I'd urge you not to panic, ironic though that sounds in a book about anxiety. Rather this is a cause for optimism, because **in tackling our fears, we're taking preventative action, helping to reduce the risk of more serious health problems and improving our sense of wellbeing in a much broader sense**.

Moreover, I'm a realist. One look at this author photo probably reveals that I'm no gym bunny; should you ever come to one of my events, you may well notice me indulge in a glass of wine. So, given I'm not likely to be entering the Olympics anytime soon, I'll keep it simple.

1.4 Medication, the options in a nutshell

There's no shame in admitting you need professional help – it's not a sign of weakness, or that you're a failure – **and if you're experiencing a lot of physical symptoms and distress, your doctor should be your first port of call.** It's important he or she checks that your anxiety isn't caused by a medical condition (such as a thyroid problem, altered blood sugar levels, or asthma). Once your doctor has ruled these out, **he or she may suggest medication.**

• **Beta-blockers** are usually associated with treatment of high blood pressure and angina, but **are sometimes prescribed for anxiety as they block the chemicals that cause physical symptoms such as sweating and palpitations.** However they won't change what's going on for you mentally.

• **Sedatives such as Diazepam act on receptors in the brain called neurotransmitters which relax the muscles.** They can make you feel less agitated and tense, but will also make you sleepy. They are also highly addictive, so should not be taken over an extended period.

• **Many antidepressants can help lessen anxiety.** Certain chemicals in the brain act as both hormones and neurotransmitters, and two of these – serotonin and norepinephrine (which is sometimes called noradrenaline) – can improve mood and emotion. Antidepressants commonly known as SSRIs (Selective Serotonin Reuptake Inhibitors) increase the levels of serotonin in the brain and tend to be what doctors prescribe first; SNRIs (Serotonin Norepinephrine Reuptake Inhibitors) increase both serotonin and norepinephrine and are likely to be prescribed only in more severe cases. Be forewarned, however; **both SSRIs and SNRIs take several weeks to**

work and you will have to be patient before you experience any benefits. There are many different types of antidepressant, and **what suits one person may not suit another**, so you may have to try more than one before finding an antidepressant that works for you. Your doctor will be able to advise you more fully on the various pharmaceutical alternatives, and there's sensible information on **www.nhs.uk**.

1.5 Making friends with your doctor

A good relationship with your GP can make a big difference to how you manage your anxiety, so it's worth pausing for a moment here to consider how to get the most out of your appointments. It's also worth remembering that it's a two-way street: how *you* act when you go for your consultation might have a positive or negative impact on your GP too. Bearing this in mind, I asked my friend Dr Patrick Fitzgerald (who co-authored *Making Friends with the Menopause* and who works as a GP in Cheshire) for some pointers. Here is what he said:

1. It's a good idea to **arm yourself for the consultation beforehand.** Bear in mind **your GP has 10 minutes to go through your concerns, examine you if necessary, formulate a plan you're both happy with and write it up.** Plus, and this can be hard if you're in a whirl of panic, try to remember that your doctor is human. He/she will be affected by the stories they hear every 10 minutes.

2. **See the right doctor**. Do you not want a specific doctor because of previous problems? Tell the receptionist. It may mean you have to wait a little longer to see the doctor of your choice, but it will be worth it in the long run.

3. Make a list. You're here about your anxiety symptoms and worries. So write them down – all of them, but stick to the subject. If you start asking about a second issue you're going to flummox the GP who has 10 minutes to try to support you with a complex problem and you're not going to get the focus you need. Make another appointment if you believe this second issue to be unrelated.

4. Tell the GP what you think may be going on. It helps establish your concerns around your symptoms and you can be reassured if you are worried unnecessarily.

5. Allow the GP to ask you questions, even if they seem irrelevant. They are sifting through information to make sure nothing untoward is going on. Smoking and alcohol information are needed – don't be upset, it's not a judgement or being nosey – doctors need this to help find the safest way forward.

6. Ask your GP what the options are. It may be medication. It may be counselling. What do you expect to happen? **Tell them what you are expecting.**

7. Make a follow up appointment, if needs be, to see how the changes have gone. Changes take time – so wait at least 2-3 weeks before checking in. If you've been prescribed anti-depressants they will take 4-6 weeks to take effect, so you may be asked to leave it longer.

8. If you feel you didn't connect with your GP, don't get angry. It may have been the consultation before yours that involved something so upsetting that they couldn't concentrate. It may be that they should retire! Make an appointment with another doctor until you find the one who suits you. Remember, your GP is there to support you. They can't fix your life, but they will listen to your worries and try to provide guidance to the best of their abilities.

Of course you may wish to manage your anxiety without the aid of conventional medicine. **You might like to investigate supplements** such as vitamin B100, St. John's Wort and Krill Oil, and Valerian and Passionflower are believed to help with insomnia. I'm not an authority on these and don't feel it's my place to encourage or discourage anyone who experiences anxiety from trying alternative cures. What I would say is that some herbal medicines and pharmaceutical products don't work well in conjunction, so it's worth checking with your GP before you combine them. (St. John's Wort, for instance, can reduce the efficacy of SSRIs.) Moreover no form of medication, conventional or complementary, will treat the underlying cause of your anxiety, so **the next step is to consider therapy.**

1.6 Therapeutic treatments, in brief

From acupuncture to yogic breathing, there many therapeutic techniques used to tackle anxiety. As with herbal medicines, many sufferers swear by complementary therapies – and I've found acupuncture helpful myself. Some find aromatherapy helps to calm them; others recommend Emotional Freedom Technique (EFT, also called tapping). Reiki healing has many advocates, so does hypnosis. However all these should be used in addition to – and not instead of – seeking medical advice from a doctor.

• I recommend that when you visit your GP, that you enquire about therapy. **Some therapies (most often Cognitive Behavioural Therapy or CBT) are available on the National Health** in the UK – though waiting times vary depending on where you live.

• **If you are fortunate enough to have medical insurance through your work or privately, you may find therapy is covered by your policy.** When you visit your doctor it's worth mentioning if you have insurance, and/or telephoning your insurer to see if your condition is covered.

• Alternatively, you may decide you wish to **consult a therapist privately who has experience of anxiety attacks and disorders.** If so, the British Psychotherapy Foundation is a useful resource of UK-accredited psychotherapists and details are at the back of this book.

In other countries such as the United States, the health system is very different, and you'll need to consult your insurer from the outset as to what your policy covers.

Whatever your circumstance, I understand all too well that if you're feeling anxious to have to wait for medication to work or for a therapeutic assessment can seem like torture – even waiting to see your GP initially can be hard. Again, I'd ask you to trust me because I've been there: you *will* get better, not least because aside from supplements and alternative therapy, **there's a huge amount you can do to help yourself. You hold the key to your own wellbeing, even though you might not feel like it right now.** So let's crack on with seeing how you can to look after yourself better, because that's what this little book is chiefly about.

1.7 The value of physical exercise

Exercise effectively:

- Burns off stress hormones such as adrenaline
- Tires your muscles, reducing excess energy and tension
- Forces healthier breathing

- Releases brain chemicals (endorphins) which are natural antidepressants
- Reduces feelings of tension, frustration and anger
- Improves sleeping, physical health and the immune system

- Provides a healthy distraction from your worries and improves overall mood

When it comes to exercise, please start slowly and sensibly. A little light jogging or brisk walking can make a big difference to your mood; spraining an ankle will have the reverse effect.

Moreover, by 'exercise' I don't just mean sports. Anything that requires you to be physically active over an extended period of time can benefit your mental health – so gardening, going for a walk with the dog, dancing and doing DIY or housework all count. Aim to build up so you do 20-40 minutes three or four times a week. That sounds doable for most of us, doesn't it?

1.8 The role of diet and drink

Eating well is associated with lower anxiety levels, fewer mood swings, and can reduce pre-menstrual fatigue.

Do:
- Eat regular meals
- Make sure you have a varied, balanced diet
- Avoid processed foods to help reduce your intake of salt and sugar
- Drink more water – drinking 2 litres a day is the quickest and easiest form of detoxification.

Don't:

- Succumb to diet/binge cycles – this will cause great highs and lows in blood sugar and is likely to lead to 'the shakes', irritability and anger
- Drink strong coffee – it often causes sleep problems and anxiety
- Drink more alcohol to ease your anxiety – we'll return to this, and other ways we self-medicate to cope with anxiety in Chapter 5.

1.8 The importance of breathing

Now onto something even more rudimentary: breathing.

Breathing gives us life: our nervous systems are driven by inhaling and exhaling, so it follows that **by changing our breathing we can influence millions of biochemical reactions in our body**. These chemicals have a major impact on us physically and mentally and many people who experience high levels of anxiety are known to breathe shallowly, through their chest. This disrupts the balance of oxygen and carbon dioxide necessary to be in a relaxed state.

By slowing the breath and inhaling more deeply, we can bring down the heart rate and reduce the amount of adrenaline the body produces, which helps us to relax.

EXERCISE
The Measured Breath

When you feel anxiety rise, practise this simple technique:

- Sit or stand, but make sure your hands are relaxed and your knees are soft
- Drop your shoulders and let your jaw relax
- Now breathe in slowly through your nose and count to four
- Keep your shoulders down and allow your stomach to expand as you breathe in
- Hold the breath for a moment
- Release your breath slowly and smoothly as you count to seven
- Repeat for a couple of minutes.

EXERCISE
Belly Breathing

Another popular technique is Belly Breathing. It's especially effective when **panic attacks** strike because it can help stop you hyperventilating or over-breathing, but it's a good idea to try it when you feel only slightly stressed so you become familiar with it. Then, if you find anxiety rising or catch yourself hyperventilating, you can start Belly Breathing immediately and it will help you feel in control, fast.

- Make sure your shoulders are down and relaxed.
- Breathe in slowly and deeply through your nose. Your stomach should expand, but your chest should rise very little.
- If you want, you can place one hand on your stomach and the other on your chest so you can feel how you are breathing.
- Exhale slowly through your mouth. As you blow air out, purse your lips slightly, but keep tongue and jaw relaxed. You may hear a soft whooshing as you exhale. Listen for that sound when you practise and learn to value it as the sound of relaxation
- Make your outgoing breath as long and smooth as you can. The exhalation is the key to relaxation, so give it your full attention
- Repeat this for several minutes.

Now you've two tools for managing anxiety that you can take with you anywhere. You don't even need a bag! Moreover, they're 100% natural, and free, and **you're making your body work *for* you, rather than against you.**

1.9 The physical changes of the menopause

In most cases, anxiety has no physical cause, but that doesn't mean that it's impossible for anxiety to be caused by physical changes, and one of the most major changes the female body goes through is the menopause. My own worst phase of anxiety hit me in my late forties, and I was struck by how many women of 'a certain age' there were in the anxiety management groups I attended back then; this is also mirrored in the membership of the *Making Friends with Anxiety Facebook* group.

Of course this is only anecdotal evidence, but it's a biological fact that in the early stages of the menopause (known as the perimenopause) levels of female hormones start to fluctuate and the shifting balance of oestrogen and progesterone can trigger emotional responses. To use a specific example, when **we flush and get hot and sweaty, it can feel alarmingly similar to the sensations of claustrophobia, suffocation and panic**. These symptoms can be frightening and when we're afraid we release more adrenaline. Little surprise that after months, even years, of being in the fight or flight mode, some women eventually collapse from exhaustion, convinced they are having a nervous breakdown – I'll admit I came close to this myself.

Given this state of affairs, it stands to reason that throughout this transition eating a diet balanced with protein, fat, and complex carbohydrates, along with moderate daily exercise is particularly helpful. (Also, if you're at this point in life, you might find reading *Making Friends with the Menopause* useful as it has a lot more detail on the subject.) But in any case, it's important to remember that whilst it may *feel* like it, the menopause is not forever. Once post menopause is reached, the turbulence of hormone imbalance will be over with all of its symptoms. Until that time, batten down the hatches, oh women readers, and be nice to yourselves.

Whatever your circumstances, **the main thing is not to fight anxiety**. When my anxiety was really bad, I fought it tooth and nail. Often I'd wish with all my heart that I could get rid of it, sometimes I'd even shout 'get out of my head!' and beat my forehead. Understanding the role of adrenaline helped me change my attitude. I realized I *couldn't* switch anxiety off, however desperately I wanted to, because it was inextricably linked to fear. Gradually, I began to appreciate it was what had kept me alive. It was the start of my making friends with anxiety and the beginning of my road to recovery.

*TIP: When I feel anxiety rising, I gently tell myself that much of what I'm experiencing is because of adrenaline and there isn't a lion about to eat me. I suggest you try similar: act normally if you can, and accept it will pass. Remind yourself it's **only** anxiety, **only** adrenaline, and that in itself it can't harm you.*

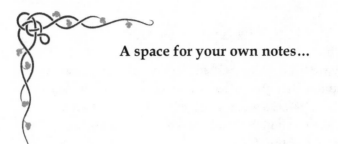

A space for your own notes...

...or just to breathe

2. 'N' is for Negative Thoughts

The way we think can heighten anxiety, so being aware of our common thought patterns and learning to challenge them can help reduce our sense of overwhelm. Becoming more objective about how others see us is also useful, as is trying to be less tough on ourselves.

2.1 Negative thinking

One of the most useful insights I gained through Mindfulness-Based Cognitive Therapy (MBCT) was that I came to appreciate that **anxious people, like me, are prone to thinking in certain ways**.

Common thoughts associated with anxiety include:

- A preoccupation with danger
- A sense of impending doom
- A fixation with getting to safety
- An inability to concentrate
- Obsessive, intrusive thoughts
- Increased sensitivity to criticism
- Negative, self-critical thoughts
- Confusion
- Forgetfulness
- One's mind going 'blank'
- A sense of unreality and disconnect from others

Some of us are more inclined to certain thoughts than others, nonetheless anxious people share a common tendency to criticize and berate ourselves, tell ourselves we're failures and useless. These thoughts can create **feelings** such as:

- Nervousness
- Terror
- Frustration
- Impatience
- Worry
- Guilt
- Shame
- Anger
- Apathy
- Loneliness
- Sadness

Feeling like this is unpleasant, which in turn tends to compound our anxiety.

2.2 Changing our minds

Until I learned about MBCT, I'd assumed there was nothing I could do to change my thinking (let alone my emotions); I believed that my thoughts controlled me, rather than the other way round. What I came to understand is that the opposite is true – **we** *can* **influence our thoughts, and if we change the way we think, then our mood will lift and, eventually, anxiety will diminish too**.

'But I *feel* it, so it must be true,' I can almost hear you muttering. It can be hard to grasp that our **thoughts are something we have power over**, so to help explain, let me share a little of my own dark past.

EXAMPLE
Many years ago, when I was a Goth, a friend, keen to see me experiment more with my clothing, suggested that I go and

get my 'colours done'. I was of the opinion I could wear 'any colour as long as it's black'; she said she'd introduce me to someone who would reveal if this was true. So at her behest, I spent an afternoon with a woman who wrapped me, at great speed, in various coloured scarves to ascertain which flattered my skin tone and hair.

Many of us have clothes we especially like; shoes we wear daily, jeans we live in, T-shirts that are almost welded to our chests. Sometimes these clothes suit us; often they're simply comfortable – what we're used to.

Sure enough, an afternoon with the scarf-wrapping woman revealed that black, in fact, did nothing for me, and when she draped me in alternative shades, I could see that bottle green and brown suit me far more. It's no coincidence it took other people to help me appreciate this: I'd got trapped in black thinking and I couldn't see a different way. But once I'd had my steadfastness challenged by this simple demonstration, a world of colour opened up to me.

Black-and-white patterns of thinking are something anxious people are susceptible to – we often polarize our opinions, seeing ourselves as abject failures or, more occasionally, big successes. But just as I was lured into experimenting with different colours, so it is with negative thoughts generally – we don't have to be so all-or-nothing about what life throws our way.

*TIP: When you wake up tomorrow, rather than think: 'I'm going to have an anxious day and feel rubbish', you could venture to consider: 'today **might** be OK after all'. Sometimes it seems like there's no alternative, but if you give it a go you might be surprised to discover there often is.*

2.3 Handling criticism

We're inclined to believe we know our own minds, so you might remain cynical that you're ever going to change yours. After all, if you're anything like me and the millions of other anxious people out there, you'll have been thinking the way you do for years, possibly decades. This is a book, not a miracle cure, and it's unlikely to change your thinking overnight, but bear with me. I will explain one area in which I used to think very negatively, and use it to show how I've managed to change my thought processes and move on. I'm *very* stubborn, and if I could do it, I've confidence you can unlock your thought patterns too.

TIP: 'I try to accept uncomfortable feelings of anxiety when they come up. I find that gently entering and exploring my feelings rather than trying to push them away gives them less power, so that eventually I can dissolve them. I also mindfully focus on things I can hear and feel, bringing me away from the story of the anxiety and back to the present moment.' Elizabeth

EXAMPLE

Earlier, I said I'd be honest, so I'll confess that taking criticism is not something I've *ever* found easy. Unfortunately, as I write novels for a living, it comes with the professional terrain. Take reviews, for instance. Although, of course, you are perfectly entitled to leave a 1* review on Amazon should you feel strongly about the quality of this book, in the past 1* reviews of my novels have been known to make me weep. From one review it's astonishing what I could extrapolate: the novel was awful – no question; I was a dreadful writer, always had been and always would be; everyone who was nice about the novel in other reviews was in fact lying; I would never write anything again, let alone anything good… I could go on.

With hindsight, it's easy to see how taking the feedback so personally and being so all-or-nothing about it created anxiety. It even led me to suffer from writer's block. I became paralysed about drafting something new, and I'm certainly not the only author to have experienced *that* very negative state of mind.

Now let me share the insight that helped give me a different – and rather healthier – perspective. One day, on the aforementioned MBCT course, the guy running it gave a group of us a simple exercise.

'I want you to picture yourself taking a lemon, putting it on a chopping board, and slicing into it with a knife,' he said.

I closed my eyes and did so, as did the rest of the group. Then he asked each of us to describe what we'd imagined.

'I took a lemon from the ceramic fruit bowl in our kitchen, and sliced it with a knife I picked from a magnetized strip on our wall,' I said.

'And the board?' he asked.

'Wooden and worn,' I explained.

'Mine was melamine,' said the woman on the sofa next to me.

'Mine was glass,' said the man opposite. Someone else was slicing lemon to make a Gin and Tonic, and so it went on.

This exercise illustrated how **we each bring our own experiences to bear on someone else's words or story.** As a writer, it helped me see that every sentence has as many different interpretations as it does readers, which

goes some way to explaining how one person's 5* book is another's 1*. There is no way I can control these responses – and nor can you if you are criticized. To try and do so is as futile as trying to control someone's thoughts.

Understanding that criticism isn't personal to the recipient, but comes from the personal perspective of the critic, can be helpful distancing us from the harshness of words and lessening their impact.

Obviously, this is only one example of changed thought processes, but from small shifts like these bigger breakthroughs can come.

EXERCISE
Dealing with criticism

Next time you feel wounded by an acid remark or criticism and feel anxiety rising as you try to control your upset, pause to reflect for a few moments. Remember this anecdote about slicing lemons and how each person sees every situation differently.

- Remind yourself things are rarely *all* good or all bad
- Consider the truth is likely to fall between 0% and 100%
- Ask if there is an opportunity for you to learn anything from the criticism offered
- As for the rest of the feedback, if it's of no use, picture yourself letting it go, like a balloon up into the sky.

'A mind is like a parachute. It doesn't work if it isn't open.'
Frank Zappa

2.4 Perfectionism

Maybe criticism from others isn't your Achilles' heel. 'I can take negative feedback in my stride,' you might say. I wonder though, do you take feedback from *yourself* so well? The idea of the inner critic – a critical inner voice – is not new. In many ways, it's a similar concept to what Freud called our 'superego' and Jung the 'animus', and often those with the harshest inner critics are perfectionists.

If you suffer from anxiety, chances are that you are obsessed with doing everything right and if you're anything like me, you probably consider it a personal strength. Well, I've got news for you: **believing you have to be excellent at all times and being anxious are often linked.** For a start, **perfectionists tend to feel even minor imperfections will lead to catastrophe**. (Believe me, I know. I'm not just the woman who has wept at 1* reviews; I once cried because I got a 'B' for an essay. I was only 12 – that's how far back *my* perfectionism goes.)

TIP: Remember that not everything you do can be to everyone's taste, and although the differences between us can cause upset, they are also one of the joys of being human.

The trouble is that being obsessed with perfection makes it scary to make mistakes, so we become fixated on checking, improving, agonising over small details. **Striving for perfection is exhausting and unrealistic, and means we're constantly setting ourselves up for failure.** Then, after spending time and effort on something, when we don't achieve an A*, we criticize ourselves, which can make us feel depressed, frustrated, angry and (sorry if I sound like a stuck record) anxious. Thus, far from being a wholly good thing, perfectionism can have a negative impact on our mental health, because *no one* can achieve A* for everything.

After all, even the greats have off days. Nadal doesn't win *every* tennis match. Clooney doesn't get an Oscar for *every* film. I'd wager even Her Majesty the Queen has days when her smiling and waving is half-hearted – there are plenty of photos when she looks grumpy. And if even the 'greats' have off-days, you might like to ask yourself what's wrong with *your* taking a few miss-steps? Being average occasionally? When people say 'be your own best friend' they're often encouraging us to be kinder to ourselves. Sometimes this involves lowering our standards, just a little. Gradually, I've come to see that I don't need to be perfect to be a success – and nor do you.

EXERCISE
Being imperfect

The trick is to learn to let ourselves off the hook. But changing old ways of doing things is hard, and feeling a failure is a very strong emotion, so I suggest starting small. Today, for instance, you could identify a task and set a time limit for it, so you can't do it perfectly.

• If you've a report or letter to write, rather than allowing yourself to take as long as you like and thus hone it to near-perfection, make yourself complete it in 15 minutes.
• Similarly, if you want to clean the house, give yourself half an hour, or five minutes per room, rather than enough time to dust and vacuum so everything is spotless.

Savour the experience as you do it, rather than being goal-orientated. Afterwards, reward yourself to mark your underachievement – enjoy the time you've saved and go out for a walk, perhaps. Or you could dine out in a new restaurant, and give yourself one more challenge: resist researching it beforehand to see how good it is!

TIP: Remember that nobody is perfect, and allow yourself to be 'good enough' rather than the best.

2.5 Common negative patterns of thought

So far, I've shared examples of my own inclination towards negative thinking and I hope that by doing so I've given you a handle how distorted and subjective our thought processes can be. What's interesting is that anxious people aren't just inclined to similar negative thoughts, but the way we think tends to follow similar patterns, too. For example:

• **Black-and-white or all-or-nothing thinking – when we polarize outcomes into extremes.** We filter out information that might cause us to perceive situations with greater subtlety, missing out on much of the colour of life.

• **Over generalising – evidence is extrapolated from an experience and an unjustified conclusion is drawn.** So we tell ourselves 'bad things are always happening to me', 'I never meet decent men' and so forth; to have concluded 'I am a dreadful writer, always have been and always will be' from one 1* review is a good example of this.

• **Self-blame** – situations are interpreted as reflecting something negative about you when they may have nothing to do with you. Thinking 'My boss hasn't spoken to me today because I'm incompetent' for instance.

• **Commanding the self** – this is very popular with the anxious. We're always saying 'I should do x' and 'I must finish y'; barking internal instructions at ourselves. Such rigidity takes little account of changing circumstance and often goes hand in hand with perfectionism.

When they're listed together like this, it's clear that many of these involve adopting a 'glass half empty' approach. Given a tendency for pessimism, it's unsurprising that anxious people often assume if we have one bad day, dozens of other bad days will follow. The irony is that this very belief serves to reinforce the experience, so gloom becomes a self-fulfilling prophecy. When I realized one bad day didn't *necessarily* lead to another it was a revelation; from then on I was able to see that a wobbly period might be a blip rather than a fast track to weeks of hell. On bad days I still find it hard to convince myself things could well get better as soon as tomorrow, but I'm less inclined to see my state of mind as permanent because, as I hope I've illustrated, if we're open and self-aware, change *is* possible.

TIP: 'I have OCD and in the past intrusive thoughts have been a distressing aspect of my condition. By far the biggest help for me has been disconnecting the thoughts from myself. So now when they come I'll say, "OK OCD, I see you. You're asking me what if I did something terrible and forgot just because that person looked at me funny," and then I move on! I'll feel the anxiety, but these days I know that it gets less with passing time, so I continue whatever activity I'm doing without letting it get to me.' Julia

TIP: Think of anxiety as someone you're in a relationship with. If you ignore, fight or try to control that person, then your relationship will be permeated by resentment, anger and insecurity and will rapidly become unhealthy. But if you respect the other person, if you're kind and accept them as they are, then the relationship is far more likely to blossom.

I'll be expanding further on how to challenge negative thoughts in Chapter 4, which looks the imagination and being focused on the future, and the roles they play in anxiety.

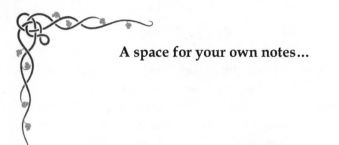

A space for your own notes...

...or just to breathe

4.   'X' is for X-factor

Whilst there are circumstances such as exams and speeches which prompt most people to worry, often what causes one person to be anxious is not a problem for another. These specific situations can be seen as the 'X-factor' – variable component – in our personal experience of anxiety.

3.1 The personal nature of anxiety

EXAMPLE

I'm hard pressed to think of a more even-tempered character than my husband, (one reason he's a good balance for a worrywart like me), and he'll merrily take physical risks I wouldn't dream of – climbing mountains, hiking across inhospitable terrain and cycling for miles with nothing but his own sense of direction to accompany him. Yet put him in the sea and it's a whole different story. Can he be cajoled to swim out of his depth? He cannot.

It's not because he's a poor swimmer – he pounds up and down our local pool with impressive strength and speed. It's because in the sea he's afraid 'there's something lurking in the darkness beneath'. A shark, a submarine, a monster with many tentacles – if I ask what's making him anxious he doesn't know. His fear can't be countered by my reasoning there are no Great Whites, U-boats or sea beasts on the South Coast of England.

Yet it's not for me to judge: as far as I know there are no man-eating moths in the UK, but nonetheless they terrify me. Unless the moth in question is very, very small, I can't be in the same room as one that's flapping around and I'll ask someone to deal with it, or scarper.

These relatively mild phobias illustrate two things: firstly, how **anxiety isn't logical**. Lots of people (even laid-back ones like my husband) have anxieties that defy rational analysis. When examined closely they're not an accurate reflection of the risk involved.

Secondly, they illustrate that **anxiety can affect how we behave**. In both cases my husband and I adopt strategies to feel safe. (He swims in the shallows, I scarper.) In other words, **even relatively mild anxiety can make us alter our actions and restrict what we do.**

Whilst my life isn't that hamstrung by my fear of moths, sometimes anxiety can make us become insular and obsessed. In the past, I've experienced bouts of more generalized anxiety, and I've become so wound up I've been unable to drive my car, meet friends or walk further than a few yards from my house. I've had to take periods of time off work, so it's worth trying to learn what triggers us and how to manage the resulting anxiety, so we can live as full and rewarding a life as possible.

3.2 Past experience and triggers

When we examine our anxiousness more closely, we can sometimes find it is set off by a past experience, so when something happens to us in the present that echoes this experience, we feel the way we felt the first time all over again. This is known as 'being triggered', and is as different for each of us as our fingerprints, as no two people have the same personal history.

EXAMPLE

I get very jumpy when people walk close behind me, and this goes back many years, to an evening when a man ran up behind me and grabbed my handbag. Rationally, I know the likelihood of being mugged again is slim – this happened 25 years ago, I've done a lot of walking since, and I've not been attacked in all that time. Nonetheless, when I sense someone is getting too near, it's as if an alarm has gone off in my head, and I often step aside and let them pass so I no longer feel vulnerable.

In this situation, I find **understanding that anxiety has a cause makes it easier to deal with the rising panic**, but at other times our responses might be hard to fathom. Some of us are triggered by rejection or criticism, others can feel panicked by people leaving or social occasions such as parties. Facebook group members mention all sorts of different fears – going to the doctor is a common one, as are dealing with banks, ex partners and making long journeys. Even everyday experiences such as making calls, opening the post and going to the supermarket or shopping mall overwhelm many of us. Yet whilst we sense all these as anxiety (with palpitations, flushing, shaking etc.), **sometimes these physical symptoms can be masking deeper emotions** such as anger, grief or sadness.

EXAMPLE

I don't know about you, but I've never been brilliant at dealing with endings. When I was 18, my parents divorced, which meant we had to move from my childhood home, but instead of getting involved and helping pack, I went on holiday. A few years later, when I wanted to finish with a boyfriend, I wrote him a letter rather than have to witness his upset face-to-face. And when I left university, I opted out of the graduation ceremony. We all have our patterns, and evidently avoidance is mine.

I'm sure I'm not alone in this. We might be more open than our ancestors, but most of us still aren't comfortable talking about death, for instance. And how often do you see rock stars continuing playing even though their glory days over and in the long-term they might be better off quitting?

The trouble with not acknowledging endings is it can leave us with feelings that haven't been expressed.

Through psychotherapy, I've come to see that it has been one of the sources of my own anxiety. For others it may lead to depression.

TIP: Take a moment to reflect on how you handle endings. Do you ignore them – like an ostrich? Flee because you're afraid? Or perhaps you get aggressive and blame others. However you tend to react, becoming aware of your patterns can be the first step towards changing them.

For 30 years my mother lived in a large farmhouse in the West Country of England, complete with roaring fire, Aga, and enough bedrooms to allow a dozen guests to stay. When my stepfather was alive they hosted huge garden parties, family gatherings, intimate dinners – you name it. And never was the house as full of love and laughter as at Christmas, when my brothers and I would drive down the motorway to celebrate with them. As we grew older, so young offspring came too, and in more recent times there were three generations enjoying yuletide together.

Sadly, a few years ago my stepfather passed away and after a while it became clear that the house was big for my mother to manage alone. In 2013 she turned 80, so it no longer seemed right that I was over two hours' away. As a result, she bought a flat and in 2014 came to live near us in Brighton. But whilst mum's new place is lovely, it's much smaller, so she can't host guests en masse.

Each family member reacted to the news that Christmas 2013 was to be our last in the ancient farmhouse differently. One niece, (then 10), burst into tears at once, while her cousin, (aged 9), told me she'd lain awake 'for hours and hours all sad' about it.

It's no wonder they were upset: the place was a large part of all our life stories. The elder one made her first cake standing on a chair to reach the work surface; the younger has spent hours sitting at the kitchen table writing and drawing.

I too was shaken by the change and, on my first night in the house over the holidays, I was too anxious to sleep. And as I lay there, I reflected on how I've dealt with endings in the past, and remembered that I usually shy away from them. It was then I decided to try something different, and to *mark* this ending. So the following morning – which was Christmas Eve – I went down to the kitchen where I found my nephew and nieces already up and writing and drawing at the table. My mother was still in bed, which made it the perfect moment.

'Hey kids,' I said. 'This is our last Christmas here in this house, so how about you each write something about your memories of it so we have a keepsake for your grandma?'

'What a great idea!' said my oldest niece. (How I love children for their enthusiasm!)

'What sort of thing?' asked the younger.

'Anything you like,' I said, not wanting to limit their imaginations. 'Perhaps we could put them all together and make Grandma a big card.'

Hours of poem-writing and storytelling, drawing and printing out photos from the computer ensued. We ended up filling not just a card, but an entire *scrapbook*.

On Christmas Day the children presented my mother with her gift. It was packed full of memories, just like the house, and it finished with a double page spread full of optimistic messages about her move and their excitement about her new home. Best of all, unlike the house, she has been able to take the book with her.

But perhaps it was me more than anyone who learned a valuable lesson that day: I don't need to run from endings. They can be acknowledged, even celebrated. Spookily, as we focused on the book, I felt my own anxiety evaporate. And, like mist clearing from a valley, it revealed a clearer view of the changes ahead. The prospect of waving goodbye to the house became less overwhelming as a result. So next time you feel inclined to avoid a funeral or dump someone by text, perhaps it's worth considering if you might behave differently. Like me, you might be surprised how therapeutic marking an ending can be.

3.4 Seeking professional help

It took several months of one-to-one therapy before I was ready to work through the situation I describe here, and in so doing I realized that my anxiety about endings was rooted in my past. I came to see that this sense of fear is connected to my childhood – my home was a source of security for me during my parent's divorce, and I was very scared to leave it, so it's not that surprising that a scenario with so many parallels should trigger me now.

When you come to facing your own fears, breaking situations down into smaller, less intimidating stages can be very helpful. We'll be coming back to this stepping-stones approach later, in Chapter 5. But before I continue, **a few words of caution: I can't unravel what's triggering you personally**. I don't know your history, and, as I've explained, I'm not a therapist. For me to suggest it's possible to ease deeper issues in a one-size-fits-all little book would be naïve and irresponsible, and **if you find you're being repeatedly triggered and it's seriously affecting your life, I'd recommend seeking professional help**.

EXAMPLE

One benefit of seeing a specialist is that you might be offered a formal diagnosis, and for some people, like Su in the Facebook group, this can be a breakthrough. 'It's only since I was finally given a diagnosis of social anxiety two years ago that I really started to understand my condition,' she says, and she has kindly given me permission to share her **tips for social anxiety** here:

- Almost everyone finds it uncomfortable to engage with strangers. It is just that for those of us with Social Anxiety, that feeling is intolerable.
- We are as important, intelligent and socially valid as strangers who make us feel small just because they are able to communicate a little more easily than we are.
- It is OK to chicken out and not go sometimes. But if we encourage ourselves to try, it is useful therapy and can help our self-esteem. If you can persuade yourself, just do it. (There is more about this in Chapter 5).
- If being in a social situation brings on a panic attack, get out of the room, sip water. Breathe steadily.
- If you are lucky enough to have sympathetic family and friends, it is OK to say 'I can't do that right now because my social anxiety is bad today'. In the long term it is better to be honest, and (unless you're an actor) it's much easier than faking illness or an appointment. ('My family can handle this, thank God,' says Su. 'But I'm not brave enough to share it with many friends yet. Having this group, where I know I can be open, helps me with that.')
- If your Social Anxiety started because people were unkind about you in the past (often it starts at school), know that you were probably just fine. **It was others own pain and insecurity that forced them to persecute you.**

Part of the work of therapy is to find out what your triggers are, and a therapist can talk with you to find out more about the nature of your anxiety disorder and devise a course of treatment. I've already mentioned The British Psychotherapy Foundation, and there are further contacts at the end of this book.

TIP: If you are triggered, try to remember that the sense of panic will pass. Nothing in life is permanent, including anxiety.

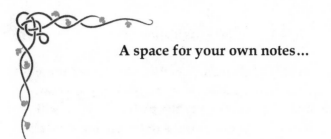

A space for your own notes...

...or just to breathe

4. 'I' is for Imagination

If the past can play a role in anxiety then so can the future; just as echoes of earlier experiences can be triggers, so can the imagination. 'If I don't go to the party, everyone will hate me' and 'if I tread on the cracks in the paving stones, then I'll have a dreadful day' are both hypothetical conclusions to draw; they're not real. Letting go of some of these perceived outcomes can be hard, but learning to see situations more objectively can help lessen anxiety.

Don't misunderstand me, **there's nothing intrinsically bad about using your imagination** – I'm a novelist so the last person likely to suggest that. It's purely that **anxious people often imagine a bleak future, not a bright, sunny one. We worry a lot about what** *might* **happen; we are filled with trepidation.**

4.1 Common imaginative patterns of thought

• **Catastrophizing** and/or **Fortune-telling** – these are similar, and involve exaggerating/predicting the likelihood of a negative event occurring. Thinking 'I can't fly to the Paris because the plane will crash' for example.
• **Mind-reading** – assuming we can read other people's minds, thoughts, intentions or motives.
• **Setting ourselves impossible goals** – using words like 'should' or 'ought' which then weigh us down.

It's easy to see how these ways of thinking can create anxiety. **To compound this, there is often direct avoidance of the feared situation,** which means our irrational beliefs remain unchallenged and therefore persist – something we'll come on to shortly.

> *'Worrying doesn't empty tomorrow of its sorrow,*
> *it empties today of its strength.'* Corrie ten Boom

4.2 Ways to tackle worry

The majority of our worries won't become actual situations and churning them over and over uses up a lot of energy, so **loosening the grip these thoughts have on us can free up our minds and lighten mood.**

'But it's easier said than done,' you might retort. 'I can't just *stop* worrying!'

Agreed, to see worrying as an activity you can switch on and off at will, like a light, is unhelpful. It's a gradual process, and **the first step is to recognize that it's happening.** There are a number of ways to approach this.

EXERCISE
Distancing yourself from worry

Let's take something you're worried about today. Now ask:

• **Is it helpful to have this worry**? Put it this way: if you're poised to take an exam, is it constructive to tell yourself you're going to fail it? Is it going to help you pass, or is it more likely to make you anxious and scared and thus affect your performance?

• **Is your worry a half-formed idea?** Many worries can be lessened by being identified properly. Write it down – often bringing it into the open will lessen its hold.

• **Is what you're worrying about true?** Look at the evidence. Again, write it down and this time, consider both sides of the argument. Remind yourself that as an anxious person, you're likely to have been thinking more negatively than necessary. Perhaps you're seeing the situation in black and white, whereas in fact there's a middle ground.

• **What is the worst possible outcome?** Sometimes voicing our worst fantasies helps us see how unlikely they are. Suppose you're worrying because you're stuck in a traffic jam and are going to be late for work. If you're like me, you won't think much beyond a general sense of panic. But if you take your worry to its logical conclusion 'if I'm late my boss will fire me' it's often possible to see we're overreacting. This last is not an approach that works for everyone – for some it may result in catastrophizing. But others may find that once we have placed limits on our worries they can be easier to deal with.

All the above involve taking a step outside yourself. **Becoming more de-centred helps us to foster a greater sense of calm and contentment.**

4.3 Insomnia and the imagination

For many of us, the early hours of the morning are when the imagination runs riot, with the result that **insomnia is a very common symptom of anxiety**. Replaying past events, feeling swamped by responsibilities – I've done them all, even though I know mulling only revs up the mind and makes matters worse.

When I was a little girl I was convinced I had 'wolves in my hair'; it was years before I realized what I could hear was the sound of my own pulse. These days my concerns are more mundane; worry about my elderly parents, dread of not getting a book finished before a deadline. Still, the imagination plays a big role. Moreover, after an hour or so, **the panic at the prospect of getting no sleep often feeds on itself, creating a vicious circle**. We tell ourselves we *should* be sleeping – surely the kiss of death for the Sandman. If you find it hard to sleep, why not try one of the following exercises, or even both?

EXERCISE
Improve your sleep hygiene

- Avoid caffeine after 1pm
- Take some gentle exercise, but not close to bedtime
- Don't have an afternoon nap
- Avoid eating a heavy meal after 8pm
- Don't drink alcohol or smoke
- Don't use a laptop or mobile phone after 9pm
- Do use a fan to block noise from inside or outside
- Before you get into bed, take a moment to pause and clear your head. Picture yourself throwing away thoughts that keep you awake. Imagine scrunching them up and putting them in the bin.

EXERCISE
Calming your thoughts

A wandering mind is often at the root of insomnia, so it can be helpful to bring your attention back to your breath, as mentioned in Chapter 1. Whether you're waiting for a lift, standing in a queue or chilling out with the dog, take a few seconds to reflect on where you are and how your body feels. Focus on a few breaths in and out, and get accustomed to letting go of your worries. The more you can do this, the easier it will be to bid farewell to your problems in the early hours of the morning and get a good night's sleep.

TIP: If you tend to view sleep as your 'due', perhaps you have false expectations. The ancients didn't get anxious about insomnia because they didn't take sleep for granted. As recently as the 18th century, it was common to sleep in two parts. Sleeping for eight hours in one go is a modern phenomenon, and I find it helpful to see my own patterns in this broader context and you might too.

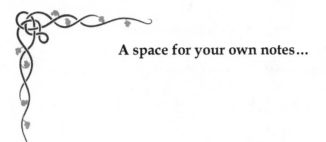

A space for your own notes...

...or just to breathe

5. 'E' is for Escalation

When we are anxious, certain behaviours are common.

- Emotional outbursts
- Restlessness
- Paralysis – like the proverbial 'rabbit caught in the headlights'
- Jumping from task to task
- Talking very fast and in a staccato fashion

Most of these are not bad in themselves. The trouble comes when you start adopting behaviours that cause your anxiety to escalate.

If we're frightened by crowds, for instance, we might stay at home 24/7, or if we're intimidated by a social event, we might drink too much alcohol to help us calm down. These tactics can offer short-term relief, but in the long run often make us feel worse. They are coping mechanisms, often referred to as 'safety behaviours', not because they *do* make us safe, but because we *believe* they do. They can end up constraining us too, so it's important to address them if we're to manage our anxiety effectively.

5.1 Common coping mechanisms

Coping mechanisms stem from the same, primitive part of the brain as the fight or flight instinct. We all have them to a greater or lesser degree, and, as with fear and anxiety, to an extent we need them. Examples include:

- **Isolation** – duvet diving, refusing to leave the house, rejecting others before they reject you

- **Running away** – cancelling appointments, avoiding situations and events
- **Seeking reassurance** – always pleasing others in case they don't like what you do
- **Immersing yourself** – in work, alcohol or drugs
- **Diversion** – generating alternative problems or focusing on someone else
- **Displacing** – where a substitute behaviour such as cleaning takes centre stage
- **Handing over** – asking someone else to rescue you
- **Procrastinating**
- **Intellectualising**

It's natural to try and stay safe, and if you can accommodate your behaviour easily, it's not something to be too concerned about. I prefer to sit on the end of the row in a cinema, for instance, but I'm not so attached to my behaviour as to be unable to sit elsewhere if a seat at the end of a row isn't free.

Thus **what's important isn't the behaviour adopted, but its depth and frequency**. If I *had* to sit on the end of the row and it meant I would miss a film if I couldn't, clearly I'd be limiting myself. Equally, carrying a tranquillizer in your handbag 'just in case' you have a panic attack is OK, but if you're having to take a tranquillizer every time you travel to work on the tube then it's become a coping mechanism, and the more you repeat it, the more entrenched the behaviour becomes. Before long the dosage of the tranquillizer will probably have to be increased in order to be effective and you're on a slippery slope to what was once helping you cope becoming a problem itself.

5.2 Drugs and alcohol

Recreational drugs and alcohol are two of the most common coping strategies – but they can also be two of the most damaging; impairing our physical health, performance at work and relationships. Drink and drugs are particularly tempting when we're anxious, but our tolerance for their effects and ability to control use may be lower, and they can interact with medications prescribed for anxiety.

Whilst many of us are aware that constructive action rather than a retreat into substance use is far more likely to help reduce anxiety in the long run, the prospect of eliminating alcohol and drugs completely can be daunting. Remember that whilst using none is ideal (particularly in the case of recreational drugs), reducing your intake is better than becoming overwhelmed and ending up back where you were. Equally, alcohol in moderation is preferable to binge drinking.

TIP: Try to recognise when you're drinking to avoid being in touch with feelings. Alcohol should be a treat, not a treatment.

5.3 Avoidance

Most coping strategies are a form of avoidance, but if we always avoid the situation, then we'll never learn we can manage it. Returning to the example of a journey on the underground; supposing as you go down the escalator you feel anxiety rising, begin to panic, and rush home. What happens is that, yes, your immediate anxiety will decrease, but also the message that avoidance helps to calm you begins to become hardwired into the brain and soon you're panicking every time you get to the tube. Because your anxiety escalates quickly and severely, this reinforces the belief you can't cope with the situation.

Once we start to avoid, the process of generalisation takes place and we end up avoiding more and more situations. So what was once a panic about one tube journey becomes a fear of any journey on the underground.

Whatever form avoidance takes – fleeing, staying in bed, over-eating, taking drugs, drinking, over-eating, you name it – the effect is the same. Maybe it's that we can't go to a party and remain sober, maybe it's that we can't leave the house without compulsively checking and rechecking the door locks a specific number of times. The interesting thing is that if we ask ourselves what would happen if we remained in the situation we're avoiding, whilst we're convinced we'd pass out, throw up, collapse, have a heart attack or some such (as illustrated by the top line in the graph here, where the level of anxiety goes up over time), actually, after a certain time, anxiety begins to decrease of its own accord (the lower line). Avoidance means we never find this out, and instead we create an endless cycle where we're trapped by our own behaviours.

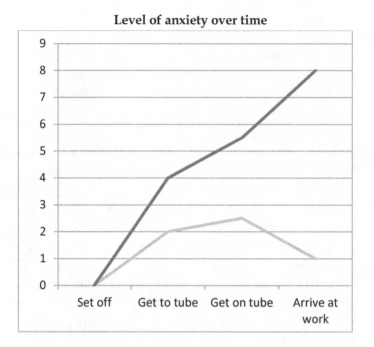

Level of anxiety over time

5.4 The vicious circle

When a therapist first explained about coping mechanisms on the MBCT course and I'd got a grasp on it, I was tempted to stand up and yell 'bingo!', I felt something so crucial had clicked into place. I realized that behaviours I thought were helping me feel better were, in fact, making me feel worse – and not just worse mentally, but physically too.

I said in the introduction I was going to talk about how **thoughts, emotions, physical sensations and behaviours are all connected,** so let's pause for a moment to see how.

The diagram overleaf shows how the ways we think affect our emotions, which in turn impact on our physical symptoms and behaviours.

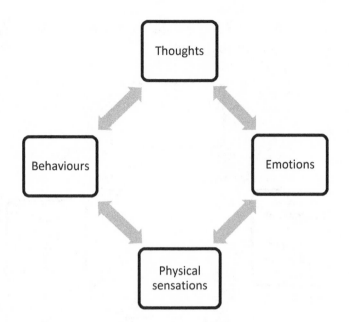

This model is sometimes called a 'hot cross bun' as we can also connect emotions to behaviours and thoughts to sensations, but I prefer to keep it simple (lest I confuse my goldfish-like brain) and the term 'a vicious circle' seems easier to grasp when we're talking about destructive habits.

EXAMPLE

When I experienced very bad anxiety a couple of years ago, my vicious circle would have looked like the diagram below. And after several weeks, it's little surprise that I became desperate and depressed. (I'm probably a good example of how anxiety can lead to depression, and why the two are often linked). Feeling like this was absolutely vile. I really think people who make light of anxiety haven't experienced it on the same level as those of us who suffer from it badly, and if you're feeling in any way similar now, you have my heartfelt sympathy.

Gradually, however, I came to understand that I wasn't helping myself. When I learned that my physical symptoms were largely attributable to adrenaline (and thus perfectly normal), I began to realize that staying in bed, far from keeping me safe, only allowed the adrenaline to keep churning round my body with nowhere particular to go.

I hope as you read about my experience you can see where we might be similar, even if your particular patterns of thinking, feeling, sensing and behaving are different. If you can recognise an overlap and substitute your experiences, with luck you'll have a 'bingo!' moment too.

5.5 Breaking the vicious circle

Back in Chapter 1, I mentioned how helpful physical exercise can be in 'using up' adrenaline, but I also pointed out that it's a good idea to take it slowly. Thus in this situation it wouldn't have been wise to jump straight out of bed and attempt a marathon. After weeks of inertia, my body wouldn't have known what had hit it, so to speak. (Not that I could run a marathon anyway, but you get my drift.) Instead, I took it slowly, getting up and doing some gentle yoga – very basic stretching and breathing. But see what happened to my vicious circle?

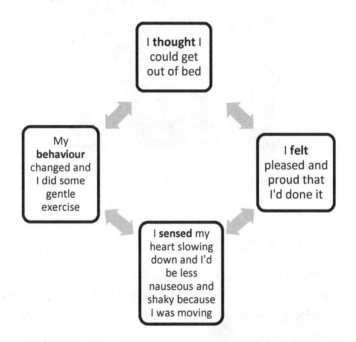

It's clearly a lot less vicious. It also illustrates why **it's important to be kind to yourself**. If I'd *not* been made aware of how destructive my thought processes tended to be, and that I could change them, I might have ordered myself 'Get up! Go out! Run 26 miles!' or something similar. But – forgive me if this sounds soppy – I was learning to be a better friend to myself, and thus it was yet another step towards my befriending anxiety.

'The first step towards change is awareness. The second step is acceptance.' Nathaniel Brandon

5.6 Changing behaviour

This helps to illustrate something else I found very helpful: that **often it's easiest to break the cycle of anxiety not by changing one's *thoughts*, but by changing one's *behaviour*, at least initially.**

By changing my behaviour (getting out of bed and doing a little gentle exercise) soon my thoughts changed, then my mood lifted a little, and my physical symptoms eased. Initially it was hard but, because they're all connected, one lead to another.

It also reinforces what I said in Chapter 1: that treatment of anxiety has to take the body into account. Until I was made aware of the physical aspects to anxiety, I remained trapped in panic and fear.

5.7 Stepping stones

There's more. This demonstrates that **tackling our fears** *gradually* **is more effective**. Supposing I *had* tried to run a marathon; it's easy to see how that particular tactic would probably have landed me right back where I'd started: in bed, heart palpitating, feeling sick and shaky. My thoughts would have been negative – 'I can't do it' – my feelings self-critical – 'I'm useless' – and so on.

Here the phrase 'walk before you can run' seems apt. If **we start slowly, then gradually, step by step, we can build our confidence and stop avoiding everything**. Sometimes this technique is called '**graded exposure**', and whether we're suffering from a phobia, social anxiety, OCD or panic attacks, the same approach tends to work well for them all. It's like taking stepping stones across a treacherous river, rather than diving straight in and hoping you can swim in a fast-flowing current.

EXERCISE
Dealing with anxiety in degrees

Take something that makes you anxious, but not terrified. Supposing you've been off work for a while, for instance, or haven't been out of the house for ages. In the case of them both the same apply:

- **Start small and take it slow** – begin with the easiest situation and practise it
- **Build up gradually** – if something is too hard, look at breaking it down into smaller, more manageable chunks
- **Be kind to yourself** – pat yourself on the back for each small step you take
- **Don't focus on how far you've got to go** or berate yourself for not getting there immediately
- **Stop before you have reached your ultimate goal**
- **Repeat** at least once a day, each time encouraging yourself to go a little further down the path.

To be most helpful, **practise should be regular, frequent and prolonged**, and you'll need to keep doing it until the anxiety has gone down, but eventually you'll make it to your destination if you're patient with yourself.

So, should you be hoping to get back to work in an office after a long break, I'd advise you to start by doing a few hours of a relatively easy task from home. Gradually build up until you feel ready to go to the office, but don't agree to start back on a full five-day week. Start on a Thursday, with two half days, and do half days the following week or two.

Equally, if you've become anxious about leaving your home, don't start by booking a trip to Timbuktu. Try doing an hour or so of gardening out at the front of your house for instance, or polishing the brass on your front door. Next, you might walk to a lamppost close by, then one further down the street, then to your local shop, and so on. One of our group members followed this advice recently, having been housebound for a year. As she said, 'If I can do it, anyone can!' and was keen for me to pass this on.

TIP: 'Feel the Fear and Do It! Beforehand, ask yourself, "What's the worst that's going to happen?" If you have that ethos it challenges the negative thoughts and when you come through your panic or fear of an event and out the other side, you can reflect and say "Well, I didn't die, didn't go mad; nothing happened like I thought it might. Yes, it wasn't nice, but I am still here." That is so empowering.' Carole

5.8 Your personal survival kit

When you're attempting to make changes to long-established patterns, **it makes sense to look after your physical and mental wellbeing as best you can with sensible preparation.** Just as we wouldn't trek up a mountain without food and water, so you might like to put together a little survival kit to help you achieve your goal. I'm not talking about slipping a bottle of whisky into your rucksack or pre-booking a helicopter so you can escape – I hope that, having read this chapter, it's clear why these coping strategies won't move you forward long term. Rather, I'm suggesting you carry one or two small items to help you remain calm. Members of the group recommended the following:

- A bottle of still water
- Tissues – helpful if anxiety makes you perspire

- A fan – handy if you often get flushed and warm
- Mints – sucking sweets such as Polos can prevent dry mouth
- Rescue Remedy – now comes as chewing gum
- Earphones – listening to music or a meditation CD can provide welcome distraction

- Copying out the mantras at the end of this book to keep in your purse or wallet

TIP: 'I'm not convinced that I'll ever be "cured" of anxiety, but now I'm better equipped to having to deal with it as I believe I'll come through it. This, plus having help 24/7 through the Facebook group, is all the ammo I need.' Debi

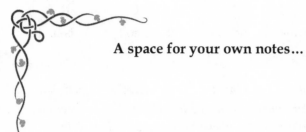

A space for your own notes...

...or just to breathe

6. 'T' is for Time

At the beginning we looked at how anxiety involves the ability to use memory and the imagination to move backwards and forwards in time. We've seen how anxious people can be triggered by past experience, and are also prone to projecting into the future and imagining the 'what ifs' of any given situation. We've also explored how this can cause anxiety to escalate. One way to break these patterns of thinking is to focus more on the present moment.

6.1 Stop the planet, I want to get off

Last September I mentioned to a friend how much I loved this time of year. 'But summer's over!' she wailed. 'Next thing I know it'll be Christmas.' Yet it was only the week after the August bank holiday. It struck me that she'd fast-forwarded through nearly four months – and with it a whole season.

My friend is not alone in ignoring the here and now – one only has to consider the high street to see how we tend not to focus on the present across our whole culture. We've autumn clothes in the shops in July, winter fashions in September and by mid-December – when one might actually want to *buy* a warm jumper – they're all on sale in preparation for spring. Talk about wishing our lives away!

When you pause to consider, it's amazing how much time we spend dreading what's not yet happened and mulling over the past, and I wouldn't be the first to point out how fruitless this is. **We can't control much of what's coming, and we certainly can't change what's been and gone**. Put like this, it seems obvious that **shifting our focus to the present will be good for our mental health,** but after years of thinking in certain ways, how on earth can we learn to do so?

6.2 Follow a furry friend's lead

Perhaps **a good place to start living more in the here and now is to channel our animal instincts.** After all, if it's true animals don't experience.anxiety like we do, doesn't it follow that in this regard we might learn from them?

Tradition has it most of us are either cat people or dog people. Even if you're neither, you're doubtless familiar with their behaviours. And (arguably because they're less intelligent than us humans – they have, so I understand, smaller brains) both cats and dogs are inclined to live in the moment. A cat is happy: it purrs. A dog wants you to throw a ball: it comes running up, wagging its tail. Neither creature (unless I'm missing something) is worried about work on Monday, or an argument they had last week with a furry friend. They just are as they are. Hungry, playful, growly, hot, sleepy. They express it, and move on. There's a lot to be said for being this way. As we've mentioned, too much living in the past and we can end up maudlin and depressed and too much living in the future can make us anxious and scared. If you want to live more in the present how about channelling some kitty or canine laissez-faire?

EXERCISE
Discover your inner pedigree pal

- You're feeling cross or frustrated? Don't brood. Express your emotions, then let them go. If you're upset, allow yourself to *feel* it – cry if you want to
- Whatever you drink today, sip it slowly
- And as you eat, savour every mouthful
- When you relax, give into the experience wholeheartedly (like our cat does, overleaf)
- Most important of all, give yourself permission not to worry so much about what's gone before or what's coming up in the next few days or weeks. After all, regretting the former or fretting about the latter won't change either, and trying to control our experiences only adds to the emotional distress they cause us
- Whatever your circumstances, try to be less judgemental and more accepting.

Again, it's a way of being kinder to yourself. And if the idea of being kind to yourself brings with it a twinge of guilt, think again of cats and dogs. Do they feel guilty about being stroked and pampered? I don't think they do.

EXERCISE
Joy

Use a pen and paper to make a list of what brings you joy right now, focusing on the present, not past or future. Pin it somewhere so you can see it, and add to it during the day.

6.3 Gaining perspective

The art of 'being present' has another benefit: we gain perspective. It's easy to lose a sense of what matters and what doesn't if our diaries comprise of long 'to-do' lists and we're constantly in a hurry to get things done. We can find ourselves cursing colleagues for not working quickly enough, sighing at strangers who get in our way and moaning when waiters don't jump to serve us the moment we've sat down.

So, next, I'd like to share another exercise – this is one I was invited to do on a yoga retreat a couple of years ago and it only takes a few minutes. What's more, it's free, and you can do it wherever you are.

EXERCISE
A five-minute wonder

At some point today, preferably in daylight hours, **take five minutes to go outside**. Leave your phone, your colleagues, your friends, ask someone to hold the baby, (though if it's raining, I will permit a brolly). The point is to go alone. On our retreat we went into an orchard to get in touch with nature, but the heart of the city will do fine.

- Now, **experience the wonder around you**. Look. Listen. Touch. Smell.
- Don't do this half-heartedly, **do it with your full attention**. See the ladybird on a leaf, a raindrop running down a window. Hear the tweet of birds, the thrum of distant traffic. Feel the damp blades of grass beneath your feet, the cool metal of a handrail. Smell the salt in the sea air, the bakery on the corner...
- **Breathe deeply** as you do this, and **every time one of your worries pops into your brain, gently push it away**, and refocus on your senses.
- Next, look up into the sky: even if it's grey, picture how far away those clouds are, and the space above them. Imagine yourself seeing the world from on high, as if from space, with Earth as part of the solar system that includes the moon, the planets, the sun.
- Close your eyes and think of the millions upon millions of stars, in a vast, vast universe, which stretches so far we can't begin to conceive it.

• Remember that **you are only one very, very small part of this universe**, just like a ladybird or raindrop, **and your worries are only a very, very small part of you.**

• In a few days, some of your worries will have passed, and even if they are still plaguing you, in the general scheme of things, given the perspective of the whole universe, they don't really matter so much, do they?

With luck, you managed to envisage some of these elements in your mind's eye. In which case, congratulations – you've been **living in the present moment**. This way of being is often called *mindfulness*, although I'll confess it took me a while to grasp why. 'But my mind is full the whole time,' I'd reason. 'So aren't I being mindful already?' Now I've come to understand that **'mindfulness' refers to the way in which living in the present moment involves filling our minds with the direct and the sensual, rather than the analytic; being less in thinking mode, and more in sensing mode**. (Or, to stick with my previous analogy, being more like a cat or dog.) **The important thing is to focus on your current experience, the here and now**.

It can be hard, if not impossible, to be like this every second of the day. We're human, after all, and as long as our memories are functioning, living a life made up of disconnected moments is simply never going to happen. Nor, come to that, would it be desirable to operate that way. But **if you can build some breathing spaces like this into your timetable, you'll be giving your mind – and yourself – a well-deserved break**. It might be a five-minute reprieve when you carry out a breathing or relaxation exercise, a walk in the park or along the seafront at lunch time or a massage after work – even all three! – but be aware of excuses you might make such as 'I'll relax when I've finished' or 'I can't stop, this is too important'.

I've done this myself, and I know there's a price to be paid. If we never stop, then eventually anxiety is likely to catch up with us. Whether it emerges as a panic attack, physical collapse, migraine or some other symptom, it'll feel like a setback, and **pre-emptive treatment is far less time consuming in the long run**.

TIP: If you find living in the present moment is proving difficult, try taking a day at a time. Focus on today's concerns, not tomorrow's. It's an extension of the stepping-stones approach. By breaking the future into more manageable chunks, it can feel a lot less overwhelming.

Alternatively, **you might like to focus on a more 'active' form of meditation – a gentle creative endeavour, perhaps, such as sewing or painting pebbles or colouring**. I confess I'm *still* not very good at focusing on breathing for more than a few minutes at a time, but give me a cushion cover to stitch or a necklace to thread and I get totally

94

absorbed, just as I did when I was small. If you're similar, you might find *More Making Friends with Anxiety: A little book of creative activities* and *A Calming Colouring Book* useful, and there are details at the end of this book.

Phew! We're nearly there. Picture these last few pages as the end of a mountain climb – we're giving ourselves one final push to the top, and then we can all relax and enjoy a glorious overview of everything we've learned. Ready?

A space for your own notes...

...or just to breathe

7. 'Y' is for You

A.N.X.I.E.T... Now we're on 'Y', the last chapter, where I'm going to focus on the most important subject of all.

YOU.

By this point you will be familiar with the main components of anxiety and the way they work together, which I hope has given you a different perspective on your anxiousness and how to manage it. Although it's inevitable you'll still experience anxiety from time to time even when you've finished this book, when you do, it's important to remember that **you have many tools to help you overcome the experience already deep within yourself.**

7.1 Being your own best friend

Returning to the notion of being your own best friend is a good way to illustrate this.

EXERCISE
A friend's perspective

Take something you're fretting about right now, and ask:

- **How would my closest friend view this situation**?
- What **advice** would they give?
- What **tone of voice** would they use?
- How much **time** would they give me?

Imagine you're talking to one another – there's no harm in actually asking and answering these questions aloud. Let's say, for instance, that you're worried about flying – many people are, and I get jittery about it myself. Would your friend say, 'Hey Sarah, yes, great that you're panicking about flying tomorrow, lots of planes crash and yours is sure to'? Would they laugh at you, tell you you're being stupid; or get angry then rush off, leaving you even more worried and unsure? If they would, then perhaps it's time to take a look at your friendship, but hopefully they wouldn't. Aren't they more likely to be kind and understanding and take time to reassure you that the odds of a disaster are very low indeed? They also might remind you that **fearing the worst doesn't make it any more or less avoidable**.

> *'The only way to have a friend is to be one.'*
> *Ralph Waldo Emerson*

Wise words, so start by being a friend to yourself.

7.2 A balanced life

You'd probably want a good friend to have a balanced life that includes plenty of room for leisure and self-care, so it's perfectly reasonable to want the same for yourself. No one wants to see someone they're fond of slave so hard they've no time for friends or family, hobbies or holidays, and most of us will have seen loved ones crumble when they've been hit by too much at once. By the same token, it makes perfect sense to make sure your own life doesn't become overwhelming. 'Prevention is better than cure', the saying goes, and it's as true for anxiety as any illness.

     Prioritizing your physical and mental wellbeing isn't anything to feel guilty about either. Keeping your body and mind healthy is not that different to making sure your car is regularly serviced or your computer is backed-up. I'd even go so far as to say that keeping yourself well is as much part of being a responsible, self-sufficient adult as other pursuits we often value more highly such as working or looking after others.

There's a lot of talk about work/life balance these days, and of course that balance looks different to each of us but consider including as many as you can of the following and your mind and body will benefit from the varied stimulation.

•   **Physical activities** – anything that requires you to be active is positive. So if deadheading all the flowers in your garden, dancing your socks off, playing ping pong or rowing down a river are what you've the urge for, go for it. Many members of the Facebook group have said that walking in nature helps them to gain perspective, and the rhythm of putting one foot in front of the other seems to break the cycle of negative thoughts. So whilst it can be tempting to stay wrapped up and safe indoors, I'd encourage you to get some fresh air if you possibly can.

•   **Creative pursuits** – whether you prefer painting or playing the piano, baking or making models, any pastime which allows you to relax is worthwhile. Self-expression is good for the heart and mind and you don't *have* to be A* level – tell that blooming inner critic to shush! If you lack confidence and are unsure of where to start, again I'd suggest the *More Making Friends with Anxiety: A little book of creative activities to help reduce stress and worry.*

•   **Socialising** – similarly, one person's perfect party is another's dreary duty, so for me to know what you'll enjoy is impossible. I do know, however, that it can be very tempting for us anxious people to persuade ourselves *not* to take the risk and put ourselves out there socially – as I've said a few times in this book. Here the phrase 'nothing ventured,nothing gained' is pertinent. It's worth reminding ourselves that a good friend is someone with whom you can

share problems, try new things, be energized, play and laugh. Put like that, is it any wonder being in another person's company can be so therapeutic?

And remember, **if you're going through a time of heightened anxiety, you might need more support.** Try to be around folk who sustain you, rather than people who undermine you – I recommend our Facebook group as a good place to start. Even if you're not someone who usually enjoys social networking, you might be pleasantly surprised by how friendly many of our members are.

TIP: 'I don't know why, but I am often the person who seems to have to look after everyone else and be the strong one, which results in there not being that many people I feel comfortable sharing my feelings honestly with. The Making Friends with Anxiety group and the friends I have made in it have changed all that. Just having my feelings heard, acknowledged and accepted, coupled together with others sharing similar or the same experiences has changed how I feel about my anxiety and how I am able to manage it.' Helen

*'With the Facebook group, it helps me not to feel so alone with it. You have a sort of instant support, just being with people who **know**. It wouldn't work if members were constant doom and gloom as I'm sure we'd pull each other under, but what I see happen is sufferers support one another with advice, experiences and friendship.'* Lisa

• **Emotional needs** – we've already touched on the way anxiety can sometimes mask unexpressed feelings, but if you're used to being seen as someone who copes it's unlikely you're going to morph into Isadora Duncan overnight, freely sharing your emotions in the form of interpretive dance.

Nonetheless, expressing yourself and how you feel *isn't* a crime, nor is it good to use drink, drugs or overeating to dull the difficulty of facing them. **Try to ventilate** instead – it's not a coincidence that talking is called a cure – and there's no reason why you shouldn't be your own therapist and verbalize your thoughts out loud.

- Shout into your pillow
- Go somewhere isolated and scream as loud as you can
- If you feel tearful, allow yourself to cry
- Alternatively, write a letter or journal.

• **Intellectual needs** – exercising the mind is as much a part of healthy living as physical exercise. It can be hard to focus on reading anything long and complicated when you're anxious (hence my keeping this book short and – I hope – sweet) but you don't need to abandon the practice altogether. I find most magazines manageable however wobbly I feel, ditto crosswords and Scrabble; for others listening to an audio book or escaping into a fantasy novel may be therapeutic. If you're feeling more robust, taking a class or course will also bring you into contact with potential friends, and it's never too late to learn a new skill.

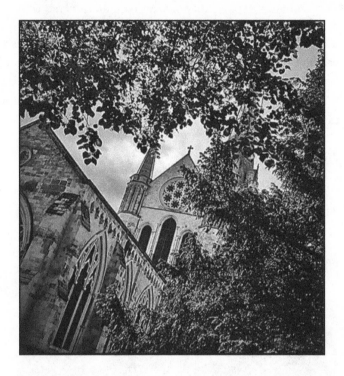

•   **Spiritual needs** – you don't need to hold formal religious beliefs to experience spirituality. Every person has their own unique sense of spirituality and different definitions abound, but if we see it in its broadest sense as **the connection between us, the world and others**, then it follows that making time for spiritual practices can help us to develop the better parts of ourselves.

- Deep reflection or meditation
  Rituals and symbolic practices
- Forms of worship

- The traditions of yoga and Tai Chi
- Enjoying nature
- Appreciating the arts
- Playing sports that involve cooperation and trust

…can all be seen as spiritual pursuits. They can help us to become more creative, patient, persistent, honest, kind, compassionate, wise, calm, hopeful and joyful and give our lives greater meaning. Which has got to be a good antidote to anxiety, surely?

7.3 A to Y, a summary of the tools at your fingertips

Yee-hah! We're at the top of our mountain. So let's take a deep breath, exhale, and enjoy the learning we've shared.

Before I finish, here's an overview of the points that make up A.N.X.I.E.T.Y., with mantras to say to yourself when the need arises. Since I published this book readers have told me they've copied these following pages so they have it with them at all times and can refer to it as part of their personal Survival Kit. You might like to do likewise.

• **Adrenaline** is what lies behind the palpitations, perspiration, racing thoughts and shaking associated with anxiety. Remember these symptoms are normal reactions and are not harmful. We need adrenaline to survive, so you'll never get rid of anxiety completely. Fighting it will make it worse; acceptance and looking after ourselves physically are the way through.

MANTRA: Resistance is futile.

• **Negative thoughts** hinder rather than help with anxiety management. Thinking how you *should* be behaving or worrying about what other people think will only make you feel more miserable. Be kind to yourself. Think positively about your abilities. No one can be perfect at everything, all the time. Being 'good enough' is plenty.

MANTRA: Don't believe everything you think.

• We all have personal triggers and situations we find especially stressful, so there's always an **X-factor** (individual component) in our experience of anxiety. Gaining greater understanding of our deeper selves through therapy can go a long way to helping us manage our reactions.

MANTRA: Our deepest wounds surround our deepest gifts.

• **Imagining** the future and worrying about all the things that could go wrong doesn't make life any more predictable – it only keeps us from enjoying the good things happening in the present. Decide what's important and try to let go of the rest.

MANTRA: 'Yesterday is gone. Tomorrow has not yet come. We have only today. Let us begin.' Mother Theresa

•   Avoidance can make anxiety **escalate** and prevent us from discovering our symptoms are not harmful. We can face our fears if we break our goals into manageable stepping stones.

MANTRA: 'Do one thing every day that scares you.'
Eleanor Roosevelt

•   The present is the only **time** that matters. Notice what's around you. Tune into the here and now. Your breath can function as an anchor to and help you tune into a state of awareness and stillness.

MANTRA: 'Stop a moment, cease your work, look around you.'
Leo Tolstoy

•   By changing the way you approach your fears, **you** can manage your own anxiety, rather than your anxiety managing you.

MANTRA: 'There is only one corner of the universe
you can be certain of improving, and that's your own self.'
Aldous Huxley

It takes trust and kindness and courage to make friends with the various anxious parts of yourself, so be gentle with your psyche.

You can't pummel your mind and body into submission, just as you can't force anyone to be your friend. Be empathetic, and take it slowly, and **remember to take your personal survival kit (see Chapter 5) with you when you're under particular stress.**

7.4 For times of need

Should there be moments when you feel panic rising and even the previous points seem too much to absorb, focus on the following:

- Reassure yourself that at some point **this feeling will pass**
- If you're just too edgy or overwhelmed with anxious thoughts to do anything other than be a bundle of nerves, **don't fight it**
- Just **sit with your feelings, accept them and focus on your breathing**
- **Remember you are not alone**
- **Believe that you will come through anxiety**
- **Because anxiety is your friend**, I promise.

'A friend is a present to give yourself.'
Robert Louis Stevenson

My thanks to you

Last but by no means least, I'd like to say thank you for reading. I hope this little book has helped unravel a complicated subject, and to lessen your anxiety. If so, I would appreciate it if you could **leave a review on Amazon.** This will help others find it and it's useful to hear what readers thought. I also suggest **you keep this book close to hand**, so if you're having an anxious day you can reach for it.

Finally, a reminder of that **Facebook group** I've mentioned so repeatedly. It's called *Making Friends with Anxiety*, and you would be more than welcome to ask to join.

www.facebook.com/groups/makingfriendswithanxiety/

In the meantime, I wish you…

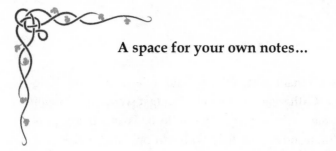

A space for your own notes...

...or just to breathe

Acknowledgements

I'd like to thank my friends and fellow authors Kate Harrison, Catherine Quinn and Bridget Whelan who all advised me on how to get this little book out there, plus Laura Wilkinson for her help with editing, Leigh Forbes for formatting the ebook, Alice Appleton with proof reading and Patrick Fitzgerald and Ian Williams for their doctorly support. My dear friend, Nicola Lowit, and my husband, Tom Bicât, read this in draft and advised me on content, and, along with Seb, my stepson, gave permission for pictures of them to be used too. I'd also like to thank all those who've worked with me in groups talking about anxiety, especially all the Admins of *Making Friends with Anxiety* online, who work tirelessly in their 'spare' time. Much of what they do is invisible to members, but it is down to them that the group is the wonderful supportive space it is.

I'd also like to acknowledge my father's input, which didn't come in the form of direct feedback, but was more profound. Eric Rayner died in 2016 but he worked as a psychoanalyst for almost 50 years. He and my stepmother, child psychotherapist Dilys Daws, have campaigned tirelessly to make psychotherapy more widely available to all. My stepmother carries on this work still and their passionate interest in mental health rubbed off on me, and their influence permeates this little book. Any inaccuracies about treatment, medication or protocol (both private and NHS) are mine, not theirs.

More about the author

Sarah Rayner is the author of five novels including the international bestseller, *One Moment, One Morning* and the two follow-ups, *The Two Week Wait* and *Another Night, Another Day.*

Friendship is a theme common to Sarah's novels, and connects her non-fiction titles too. In 2014 she published this book, *Making Friends with Anxiety*, and it was followed by *More Making Friends with Anxiety*, *Making Friends with Anxiety: A Calming Colouring Book* with illustrator Jules Miller, *Making Friends with the Menopause* and *Making Friends with Depression* with Kate Harrison and Dr Patrick Fitzgerald. In 2017 Sarah set up a small press, Creative Pumpkin Publishing, and you can find out more at www.creativepumpkinpublishing.com.

Sarah lives in Brighton with her husband, Tom, and stepson, Seb. You can hook up with her on Facebook, on Twitter and via her author website, www.sarah-rayner.com, where you can sign up for her mailing list and to receive her *Making Friends* magazine with a free short story and mood-boosting guide.

Making Friends with Depression: A warm and wise companion to support you through dark times

From the bestselling authors of *Making Friends with Anxiety* and *The 5/2 Diet Book* comes a clear and comforting book to help sufferers of depression.

If you're suffering from depression or low mood, you can end up feeling very alone, desperately struggling to find a way through, but recovery *is* possible and bestselling authors Sarah Rayner and Kate Harrison, together with GP Dr Patrick Fitzgerald show you how. They explain that hating or fighting the 'black dog' of depression can actually prolong your suffering, whereas 'making friends' with your darker emotions by compassionately accepting these feelings can restore health and happiness.

Sarah and Kate write with candour, compassion and humour because they've both been there and, together with Dr Patrick Fitzgerald, have produced a concise and practical guide to help lift low mood and support the journey to recovery. It explains:

* The different types of depressive illness
* Where to seek help and how to get a diagnosis
* The pros and cons of the most common medications

* The different kinds of therapy available
* Why depression can cause so many physical symptoms
* What to do if you suffer suicidal thoughts
* How to stop the spiral of negative thinking
* The link between poor self-esteem and depression
* And why hating depression can make it much worse

Fully illustrated by Sarah Rayner and reflecting the latest National Institute for Health and Care Excellence guidelines, *Making Friends with Depression* is much more than a memoir; it aims to help you see how depression can feed on itself and show you ways to break that cycle by treating your body and mind with understanding and kindness. You'll find realistic suggestions on eating and exercise, advice on self-medicating with drink and drugs, as well as tips on reaching out and avoiding relapse, all delivered with a surprising lightness of

touch. The result is book that doesn't shy away from the bleakness or difficulties of the subject but remains tender and life-affirming, offering hope and guidance through the darkest of times.

Out now on Amazon: Paperback £4.99, ebook £1.99

More Making Friends with Anxiety: A little book of creative activities to help reduce worry and panic

If you enjoyed *Making Friends with Anxiety*, why not take a look at *More Making Friends with Anxiety*, the follow-up to the word-of mouth success?

In *More Making Friends with Anxiety*, Sarah Rayner explores the importance of 'making friends with anxiety' in even greater depth, and explains how gentle creative activity can help. It's packed with easy, practical things to make and do which will occupy your hands and calm your mind:

* Paint Pebbles * Decorate glass * Make a Collage
* Sew a Simple Cover * Bake a Crumble * Carve Wood
* Plant a Windowbox * Make a Necklace * Look at Art
* Listen to Music … and more

Written with Sarah's trademark warmth and humour, *More Making Friends with Anxiety* is filled with an array of cheap and easy activities that will inspire and uplift you, nurturing mindfulness and positivity. And because each project can be completed in less than two hours, they're ideal for complete novices and children too.

* Fully illustrated, with photographs by the author and clear step-by-step instructions

* A fantastic 'next step' for people who enjoy colouring books, offering new and exciting creative activities

Out now on Amazon: Paperback £3.99, ebook £0.99

Rated 4.9*s on Amazon

Making Friends with Anxiety:
A Calming Colouring Book

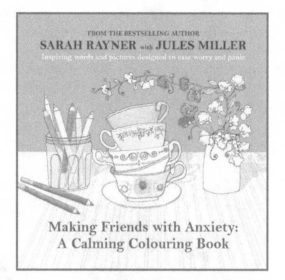

A beautiful adult colouring book packed with tips and insights to encourage mindfulness and ease worry and panic.

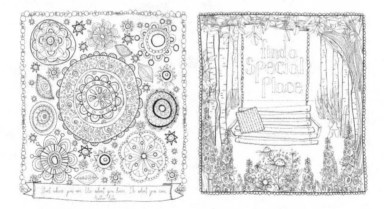

Out now on Amazon in paperback £3.99 Rated 4.6*s

Alongside a series of beautifully-crafted pictures, Sarah Rayner explains with warmth and humour how to 'make friends with anxiety' and thereby manage stress. She shows why some of us are prone to anxiety and why colouring, in particular, can be so therapeutic. She then explores other creative activities that can have a similar effect on the psyche, providing readers with a wide array of solutions that encourage mindfulness and help reduce worry.

This text is offset by Jules Miller's detailed illustrations designed to maximize the pleasure of zoning out from day-to-day worries and becoming absorbed in colouring. There are abstract patterns and cheery animals, gorgeous flowers and quirky landscapes, and each picture incorporates a 'mantra' – a few simple words to reflect upon and help boost your mood whenever you look at it. The result is a book to treasure – a unique combination of wit and wisdom that can encourage positivity long after the colouring is done.

Making Friends with the Menopause: A clear and comforting guide to support you as your body changes

Out now on Amazon Paperback £6.99, ebook £1.99 Rated 4.6*s

Many women consider the menopause anything but a friend, but together with Dr Patrick Fitzgerald, Sarah Rayner explains why rather than fighting or ignoring the changes our bodies go through, understanding the experience can help us feel a whole heap better.

Just why does stopping menstruating cause such profound hormonal shifts in the body, leading us to react in myriad ways physically and mentally? Here you'll find the answers, along with practical advice on hot flushes and night sweats, anxiety and mood swings, muscular aches and loss of libido, early-onset menopause, hysterectomy and more, plus a simple overview of each stage of the process so you'll know what to expect in the years before, during and after.

FICTION BY SARAH RAYNER

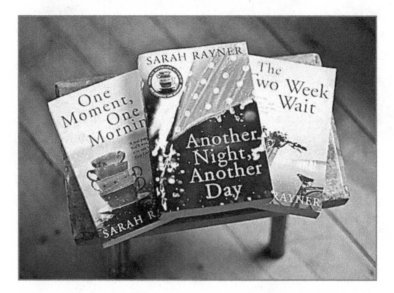

One Moment, One Morning

'*Delicious, big hearted, utterly addictive… irresistible*' **Marie Claire**

'*A real page-turner… You'll want to inhale it in one breath*' **Easy Living**

The Brighton to London line. The 07:44 train. Carriages packed with commuters. A woman applies her make-up. Another observes the people around her. A husband and wife share an affectionate gesture. Further along, a woman flicks through a glossy magazine. Then, abruptly, everything changes: a man has a heart attack, and can't be resuscitated; the train is stopped, an ambulance called. For three passengers on the 07:44, life will never be the same again…

The Two Week Wait

'*Carefully crafted and empathetic*' **Sunday Times**

'*Explores an emotive subject with great sensitivity*' **Sunday Express**

After a health scare, Brighton-based Lou learns that her time to have a baby is running out. She can't imagine a future without children, but her partner doesn't feel the same way. Meanwhile, up in Yorkshire, Cath is longing to start a family with her husband, Rich. No one would be happier to have a child than Rich, but Cath is infertile. Could these two women help each other out?

Another Night, Another Day

'*An irresistible novel about friendship, family and dealing with life's blows*' **Woman & Home**

'*A sympathetic insight into the causes and effects of mental ill-health as it affects ordinary people. Powerful*' **My Weekly**

Three people, each crying out for help . . . There's Karen, worried about her dying father; Abby, whose son has autism and needs constant care; and Michael, a family man on the verge of bankruptcy. As each sinks under the strain, they're brought together at Moreland's Clinic. Here, behind closed doors, they reveal their deepest secrets, confront and console one another and share plenty of laughs. But how will they cope when a new crisis strikes?

Useful websites

Anxiety:
www.anxietyuk.org.uk
www.supportline.org.uk
www.socialanxietysupport.com

Counselling:
www.britishpsychotherapyfoundation.org.uk/
www.counselling-directory.org.uk

Mental health:
www.mentalhealth.org.uk
www.mind.org.uk
www.moodscope.com
www.rcpsych.ac.uk (Royal College of Psychiatrists)
www.rethink.org
www.actionforhappiness.org
sane.org.uk
www.time-to-change.org.uk

Addiction – www.alcoholics-anonymous.org.uk
Alzheimer's – alzheimers.org.uk
Bereavement – www.cruse.org.uk
Bipolar disorder – www.bipolaruk.org.uk
Depression – www.depressionalliance.org;
PTSD – www.ptsd.org.uk
Suicide – metanoia.org; www.samaritans.org (08457 909090)
Tourette's – www.tourettes-action.org.uk

General health:
www.bupa.co.uk
www.childline.org.uk
www.netdoctor.co.uk
www.nhs.uk
www.patient.co.uk

Recommended reading

Anxiety:

The Feeling Good Handbook, David D Burns

Overcoming Social Anxiety & Shyness, Gillian Butler

Overcoming Insomnia and Sleep Problems: A Self-Help Guide Using Cognitive Behavioural Techniques, Colin A. Espie

Anxiety: Panicking about Panic: A powerful, self-help guide for those suffering from an Anxiety or Panic Disorder, Joshua Fletcher

Feel The Fear And Do It Anyway: How to Turn Your Fear and Indecision into Confidence and Action, Susan Jeffers

My Age of Anxiety, Scott Stossel

Bereavement:

Grief: On Grief and Grieving: Finding the Meaning of Grief Through the Five Stages of Loss, Elisabeth Kubler-Ross David Kessler

Depression:

Shoot the Damn Dog, a memoir of depression, Sally Brampton

Depression, The curse of the strong, Dr Tim Cantopher

The Unquiet Mind, a memoir of moods and madness, Kay Redfield Jamison

Sunbathing in the Rain, a cheerful book about depression, Gwyneth Lewis

Dementia and Alzheimer's Disease:

The Forgetting David Shenk

Mindfulness and CBT:

Mind Over Mood: Change How You Feel By Changing the Way You Think, Beck, Greenberger and Padesky

Full Catastrophe Living, how to cope with stress, pain and illness using mindfulness meditation, Jon Kabat-Zinn

Sane New World, taming the mind, Ruby Wax

Mindfulness, A practical guide for finding peace in a frantic world, Mark Williams and Danny Penman

The Mindful Way Through Depression, freeing yourself from chronic unhappiness Mark Williams, John Teasdale, Zindel Segal and Jon Kabat-Zinn

General Mental Health:

What's Normal Anyway? Celebrities own stories of Mental Illness, Anna Gekoski and Steve Broome

The Examined Life, how we lose and find ourselves, Stephen Grosz

Please also see my website, **www.thecreativepumpkin.com**, where there's more detail on several of these titles.

Related articles

Anxiety:

http://www.dailymail.co.uk/femail/article-2614530/The-midlife-crisis-anxiety-epidemic-Palpitations-constant-fear-crippling-panic-attacks-chronic-anxiety-wrecking-lives-generation-women-live-for.html (includes my own story)

http://www.newstatesman.com/2014/04/anxiety-nation-why-are-so-many-us-so-ill-ease

http://www.telegraph.co.uk/health/wellbeing/11046587/How-to-detox-your-life-beat-anxiety-through-meditation.html

http://www.theguardian.com/society/2013/sep/15/anxiety-epidemic-gripping-britain

http://www.dailymail.co.uk/health/article-32984/How-treat-anxiety.html

Panic attacks:

http://www.dailymail.co.uk/health/article-2156928/How-control-panic-attacks.html

http://www.huffingtonpost.com/julie-sacks/personal-health-_b_5673365.html

Insomnia:

http://www.theguardian.com/lifeandstyle/2014/apr/19/tips-to-combat-insomnia

Mindfulness:

http://www.theguardian.com/lifeandstyle/2014/jan/11/julie-myerson-mindfulness-based-cognitive-therapy http://www.psychologytoday.com/blog/urban-mindfulness/201106/mindfulness-and-anxiety-interview-dr-lizabeth-roemer

Depression:

http://www.nytimes.com/2014/08/16/opinion/depression-can-be-treated-but-it-takes-competence.html

http://www.theguardian.com/commentisfree/2014/aug/20/men-suffer-depression-anxiety

http://www.huffingtonpost.co.uk/jamie-flexman/depression-mental-illness_b_3931629.html

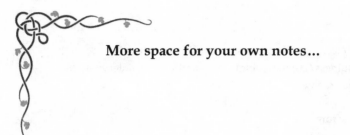

More space for your own notes...

The End